The Future of Africa:
A New Order in Sight?

Jeffrey Herbst and Greg Mills

ADELPHI PAPER 361

Oxford University Press, Great Clarendon Street, Oxford OX2 6DP
Oxford New York
Athens Auckland Bangkok Bombay Calcutta Cape Town
Dar es Salaam Delhi Florence Hong Kong Istanbul Karachi
Kuala Lumpur Madras Madrid Melbourne Mexico City
Nairobi Paris Taipei Tokyo Toronto
and associated companies in Ibadan

Oxford is a trade mark of Oxford University Press

Published in the United States
by Oxford University Press Inc., New York

© The International Institute for Strategic Studies 2003

First published November 2003 by **Oxford University Press** for
The International Institute for Strategic Studies
Arundel House, 13–15 Arundel Street, Temple Place, London WC2R 3DX
www.iiss.org

Director John Chipman
Editor Tim Huxley
Copy Editor Richard Jones

British Library Cataloguing in Publication Data
Data available

Library of Congress Cataloguing in Publication Data

ISBN 0-19-853040-4
ISSN 0567-932x

Contents

5   **Introduction** Western Concerns and African Initiatives

11   Chapter 1 **The African Development and Security Record**
- *The overall record is poor 11*
- *Growing heterogeneity 16*
- *Size counts 17*
- *Assessing Africa's insecurities … 21*
- *… and the impact on the West 25*

29   Chapter 2 **Western Responses to Africa's Crisis**
- *The endless search for African partners 34*
- *Energetic conservatism 37*

41   Chapter 3 **Paradox and Parallax:**
The Special Case of South Africa?
- *Political parallax and economic delivery? 42*
- *South Africa's foreign policy: a bridge for the West in Africa? 43*

49   Chapter 4 **NEPAD and the AU: Towards a New Order?**
- *NEPAD in detail 50*
- *The need for roll-out and momentum 57*
- *Regional integration and insecurity 59*
- *Business and government 62*

65   Chapter 5 **Tasks for the Future**
- *The aid Africa needs 66*
- *The trade Africa needs: what the West can do for Africa 68*
- *The security Africa needs: what Africa can do for itself 70*
- *The states Africa needs 71*
- *The leadership Africa needs 75*

77   **Conclusion** Zeitgeist and Realism

81   **Notes**

Glossary

ADB	African Development Bank
AGOA	African Growth and Opportunity Act
ANC	African National Congress
APRM	African Peer Review Mechanism
AU	African Union
CSSDCA	Conference on Security, Stability, Development and Co-operation
COMESA	Common Market for Eastern and Southern Africa
COSATU	Congress of South African Trade Unions
DBSA	Development Bank of Southern Africa
EAC	East African Community
ECA	Economic Commission for Africa
ECOSOC	the UN Economic and Social Council
ECOWAS	Economic Community of West African States
EU	European Union
FDI	Foreign Direct Investment
FRELIMO	Frente de Libertacao de Mocambique
IGAD	Inter-Governmental Authority for Development
MPLA	Movimento Popular da Libertacao de Angola
NAM	Non-aligned Movement
NEPAD	New Partnership for Africa's Development
OAU	Organisation of African Unity
OECD	Organisation for Economic Co-operation and Development
RCD	Rally for Congolese Democracy
RENAMO	Resistencia Nacional Mocambicana
REPAs	Regional Economic Partnership Arrangements
RUF	Revolutionary United Front
SACP	South African Communist Party
SADC	Southern African Development Community
UMA	Union of Arab Maghreb
WCAR	World Conference against Racism, Racial Discrimination, Xenophobia and Related Intolerance
WSSD	World Summit on Sustainable Development
ZANU-PF	Zimbabwe African National Union-Patriotic Front

Introduction
Western Concerns and African Initiatives

In an age of unprecedented global prosperity, 40% of Sub-Saharan Africa's 600 million people exist on less than $1 per day, and one-third of its 53 states are affected by conflict. Today, average per capita income in Sub-Saharan Africa is lower than it was 20 years ago, and human development, as defined by the *Human Development Report,* has actually declined in recent years.[1] However, following ceaseless warnings of Africa's marginalisation, the continent's development prospects are once again receiving considerable international attention. Development in Africa is almost universally recognised as one of the major problems confronting the world in the twenty-first century.

This acknowledgement is not motivated simply by altruism, however. The events of 11 September 2001 have underscored the importance of African development – and the security of Africa's peoples. There is a global consensus that Africa's failure to develop threatens not only the future of hundreds of millions of people on the continent itself but also that it is an international problem. The region's continued impoverishment may provide a reservoir for HIV/AIDS and a sanctuary for terrorists, as well as resulting in endless demands for humanitarian assistance. From the unconventional May 2002 tour of Africa by then US Treasury Secretary Paul O'Neill and the rock star, Bono, to the June 2002 G8 summit in Kananaskis, Canada, it is clear that the world is searching for answers to prevent Africa from falling even further behind.

US President George W Bush's National Security Strategy, released on 19 September 2002, recognises the danger posed by poverty, weak states, and, most important of all, global indifference and inaction. It points out that:

> *The events of September 11, 2001, taught us that weak states,
> like Afghanistan, can pose as great a danger to our national
> interests as strong states. Poverty does not make poor people
> into terrorists and murderers. Yet poverty, weak institutions
> and corruption can make weak states vulnerable to terrorist
> networks and drug cartels within their borders.* [2]

The Strategy proposes a number of ways to remedy this situation, including:

- implementing regime change in rogue states;
- the use of ad-hoc 'coalitions of the willing', as the preferred means of addressing international security threats;
- economic- and political-assistance programmes to counter the problem of failing states;
- support for key allies, including in Africa, Kenya, Ethiopia, Nigeria and South Africa;
- the use of pre-emption as a tool to tackle insecurities.

But this Strategy raises at least as many questions as it does answers.[3] Importantly for Africa, there is little in the way of detailed initiatives to solve the problem of failing states, and the relationship between such entities as 'roguehood', democratisation and development is not well defined. There is little clarity in terms of the model needed to achieve what the strategy denotes as 'national success', beyond the generalities of 'freedom, democracy and free enterprise'. How might this be encouraged in relation to existing orders (and even grafted on to them)? And how might the pursuit of national success be reconciled with US support for undemocratic and sometimes repressive allies?

The Strategy does, however, point to fundamental problems related to security and state weakness in Africa. By the start of the twenty-first century, latent or open hostilities were affecting Angola, Burundi, Cameroon, Chad, Côte d'Ivoire, the Democratic Republic of Congo (DRC), Djibouti, Eritrea, Ethiopia, Guinea, Guinea–Bissau, Kenya, Liberia, Nigeria, the Republic of Congo, Rwanda, Senegal, Sierra Leone, Somalia, Sudan, Tanzania–Zanzibar, Uganda and Zimbabwe.[4] The United Nations (UN)[5] estimated that, by 2003, 23 countries in Sub-Saharan Africa 'were experiencing some kind of [conflict] emergency', resulting in 'several hundreds of thousands of deaths, especially of children and women, vast population movements, malnutrition, and the wider propagation of diseases such as HIV/Aids, tuberculosis, malaria, acute respiratory infections and intestinal disorders, not to mention sheer human suffering, and several other communicable and non-communicable diseases, including mental illnesses'. More than 3.5m of the 14m-plus refugees and asylum seekers in the world were in Africa; of the estimated 21m internally displaced people worldwide, more than ten million are Africans; and 120,000 child soldiers, out of a global total of 300,000, are said to be participating in various African wars. It is calculated that wars are costing Africa $15 billion per year.

African states' propensity to engage in war as a means of settling differences reflects, inter alia, weak, imperfect and mutating state formations, porous and unregulated borders, absence of effective institutions, a hostile international economic environment that often discriminates against the continent's exports, insufficient technical and human skills and capacity, and easy availability of weapons. Wars have also been prolonged by the abuse of natural resources, including diamonds and oil.

Persistent conflict reflects Africa's inability to benefit at a desirable rate from globalisation. Indeed, the ability of African states to provide for their citizens has not, it would appear, improved with the spread of globalisation – in the form of increased capital and trade flows and debt reduction. In fact, as will be noted in detail, African states have, on average, become increasingly marginalised from the world economy, with their share of global trade and capital falling during the 1990s from 7% and 6% respectively in 1950 to 2% and 1% today. In the 1980s, Africa received around 30% of global foreign direct investment (FDI) in developing countries; today it receives approximately 7%.

In summary, Africa's wars have their roots in a complex compendium of social, leadership, resource, personality, class, ideological, colonial, post-colonial, ethnic, territorial, religious and Cold War divisions. These vary in type, combination and intensity from country to country and region to region. Problems of state legitimacy are related to weak political systems, characterised by insufficient checks and balances. The result is that, in many cases, an already weak state has been further undermined or has collapsed as a consequence of a vicious cycle caused by a shortage of skills, poor management, leadership abuse, and even war itself.

Yet, there are important new African-led initiatives that seek to give Africans greater control over their destiny and to take advantage of the world's attentiveness to its poorest continent. Two recent events offer a glimpse of a more promising African future: the creation of the New Partnership for Africa's Development (NEPAD) in 2001; and the birth of the African Union (AU) in 2002. Along with global economic recovery and the fight against terrorism, a new plan for African reconstruction in conjunction with industrialised countries – NEPAD – was top of the agenda at the G8's Kananaskis summit. NEPAD targets annual African investment of $64bn to achieve economic growth rates above 7% to reverse Africa's economic decline and to arrest poverty. It recognises that Africa must establish peace, good governance and effective policy if it is to meet its major development challenges.

NEPAD was received with some enthusiasm at Kananaskis. Indeed, the deference the leaders of the industrialised countries showed to South African President Thabo Mbeki and the co-architects of NEPAD, including Nigerian President Olusegun Obasanjo, suggested just how much Africans had managed to alter the tenor of global thinking since Africa was labelled by *The Economist* as 'The Hopeless Continent' in May 2000.[6] NEPAD has also successfully changed the nature of the African development agenda: 'partnered' and mutually beneficial sustainable development has replaced increasing aid dependency. The commitments to good governance embodied in NEPAD would have been unthinkable gestures on the part of African leaders even just ten years ago. The importance of these shifts should not be underestimated.

The African Union which succeeded the Organisation of African Unity (OAU) in July 2002, is intended, in part, to mark a new beginning, as Africans become less concerned with problems associated with the end of colonialism and more focused on the issues that they confront in the early twenty-first century. A positive start has been made with regard to progress in ending conflicts in Angola, the DRC and Sudan. However, fresh violence in Côte d'Ivoire in late 2002 and the continuing catastrophe in Zimbabwe demonstrate how much more needs to be done. That two of the African states previously considered to be among the most solid and prosperous are now bordering on collapse reveals just how high the stakes are for the AU.

Now is, therefore, an especially appropriate time to examine the prospects for African development and conflict resolution and to assess the viability of the proposals put forward by African countries. Does NEPAD represent an approach that could at least provide some hope of ending Africa's extraordinarily poor economic performance? And do NEPAD and the AU constitute a new approach to conflict resolution? Will NEPAD have a marked impact on the quality of political, economic and corporate governance in Africa? Or are NEPAD and the AU two more grand proposals born with great fanfare but destined for an early death? While the dangers of proclaiming that this is Africa's last chance to reverse its fortunes are clear, NEPAD and the AU have emerged at a particularly significant time, as Africans and the industrialised countries search for new answers to the continent's chronic problems. If these formulations do not work, it will be even harder for the continent to change its lot in future.

This paper first provides a brief review of African development and security over the past three decades, with special emphasis on the increasing heterogeneity of Africa. It focuses on the downward spiral in state capacity caused by declining economic fortunes and growing rebel threats, especially in large African countries, which have never had a tradition of controlling their territory. The paper also assesses progress made by the continent's superpower, South Africa, since 1994, and the role that it might play in Africa as a partner of the West and as a promoter of African reform and recovery. It then describes current Western approaches to Africa, focusing on the opportunity for countries south of the Sahara to develop comprehensive new ideas to tackle their structural problems. Next it reviews NEPAD and the AU to gauge their potential to take advantage of Western policies and, fundamentally, to address Africa's structural problems. Finally, the paper suggests what must be done in order for African countries to reverse their growth and security trajectories and asks if any African country will be able to establish the prerequisites for sustained high-level growth.

Chapter 1

The African Development
and Security Record

Numerous excellent studies have documented the economic challenges facing Africa, the profound negative consequences of low growth for Africa's peoples, and the increasing role that conflict has played in thwarting the continent's ambitions.[1] Rather than provide yet another analysis of the African economic experience, this paper examines three trends which are especially important to understanding Africa's development experience, the relationship between security and development, and the likely viability of the NEPAD proposals.

The overall record is poor

A critical first observation concerns Africa's poor growth, in absolute and relative terms, particularly since the late 1970s. Per capita growth in the 1960s was positive and, in retrospect, impressive, although it was held at the time to be inadequate. With the benefit of hindsight, it is clear that African countries, as commodity producers, generally benefited from the sharp upswing in raw-material prices in the 1970s, when the price of oil (an important export for a few African countries) increased dramatically and when the prices of other commodities rose due to the fear that many cartels could develop.

However, when the Shah of Iran was deposed in 1979, the subsequent further dramatic increase in the price of oil had an overall harmful effect on Africa. Soon thereafter, the price of oil itself began to decline, along with other commodity prices. At the same time, poor economic policies adopted shortly after independence were beginning to have a profound impact on a number of countries. It was becoming

Graph 1 GDP Per Capita in Sub-Saharan Africa (constant 1995 US$)

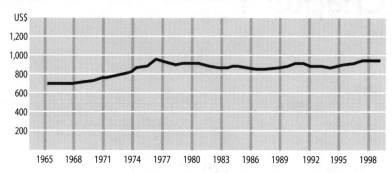

Source: World Bank, *World Bank Africa Database 2002* on cd-rom
(Washington, DC: The World Bank, 2002).

obvious that many economies had 'hollowed out', as investors slowly opted to flee.

As a result, beginning in the mid-1980s, prompted by the imposition of increasing conditions by the International Monetary Fund (IMF) and the World Bank, many African countries embarked on a halting programme of economic reform, encompassing, for instance, devaluation of grossly overvalued currencies, reduction of government deficits, reform of parastatals, and changes in the way that farmers were paid. While these reforms were necessary, it soon became apparent that they were often not credible and did not go far enough because of poor governance in many countries. Therefore, subsequent reform efforts, often impelled by conditions attached to bilateral and multilateral assistance, focused on increasing the independence of central banks, reforming the civil service to make it smaller and more efficient, improving judicial systems so that countries could protect property rights, reforming the police so that they could fight crime, and improving the allocation of social services to take account, especially, of the critical role of women in development. Finally, the wave of political liberalisation that swept across Africa from the early 1990s also raised fundamental questions about democracy, voting rules, self-determination of minority groups and human rights.

Consequently, since the early 1980s, African countries have been involved in a series of debates that have questioned, at one time or another, almost every internal practice and policy of the state. Given how difficult and controversial many of these reforms have been, implementation has been a faltering and extremely uneven process.

A continental scorecard would show that there has been some improvement in macroeconomic performance (especially the elimination of overvalued exchange rates), less success on the more difficult issues of improving governance, and slow progress on democratisation. Of course, two decades is hardly a long time given the ambitious nature of the reform proposals; however, Africa's desperate economic situation makes the reforms urgent.

There was, in fact, a brief growth spurt in the early 1990s, propelled by the devaluation of the CFA franc and other policy reforms. However, the wars that engulfed much of Africa in the late 1990s (notably in Angola, the DRC, Ethiopia and Eritrea, Liberia, Sierra Leone and Sudan) erased the fragile gains of the previous few years. Hence, despite many policy initiatives in the 1980s and 1990s, Africa as a whole has never managed to return to the (relative) high point of the late 1970s.

Africa's disappointing performance in comparison to other regions is evident from the chart below. The Middle East and North Africa, and East Asia and the Pacific – both of which were poorer than Africa in the early 1960s – have exceeded it in relation to absolute per capita.

South Asia, a region that was significantly poorer than Africa in the early 1960s, has now almost caught up and probably will surpass Africa given its distinct positive trajectory. More generally, questions posited about African development are increasingly different to those asked about other regions. During meetings of leaders of East Asia or

Graph 2 GDP Per Capita Over Time (constant 1995 US$)

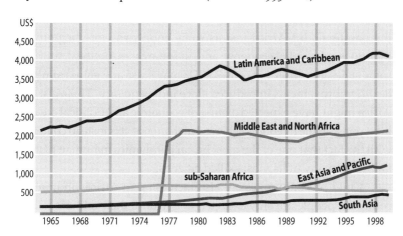

Source: World Bank, *World Development Indicators 2001* on cd-rom (Washington, DC: The World Bank, 2001).

Graph 3 Illiteracy Rate (percent)

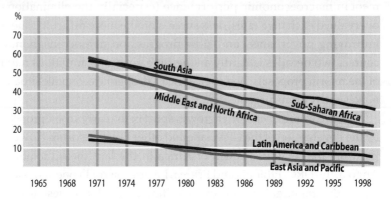

Source: World Bank, *World Development Indicators 2001*.

Latin America, development debates centre on attracting foreign investors and making local industry more competitive. For a large number of African countries, basic development questions now revolve around institutional survival rather than success in the new global economy.

As is by now well known, all of Africa's development indicators reflect its poor economic performance. There has, of course, been some progress in African development over the past four decades. But the victories have been hard won and the achievements are often frail, not as impressive as in other developing countries, and, given the overall environment of profound scarcity and conflict, always vulnerable to reversal. Indeed, one of the worst effects of the HIV/AIDS crisis is that the pandemic hit Africa just as some countries were beginning to introduce substantial economic and, in some cases, political reforms. In some states, the virus that causes AIDS may erase any gains from public health improvements introduced since independence. Thus, just when Africa might have expected a burst of economic and political creativity in response to the freedoms achieved in the 1990s, it is instead contending with the fact that one of the most brutal pandemics in human history is killing off many of its most skilled citizens.

Child mortality rates are also increasing in Africa, and, in some countries, people are only expected to live until their mid-40s.

Africa's growth record is particularly disappointing in view of the extremely generous level of foreign assistance that it has been awarded. As the chart on Aid per Capita (page 16) makes clear, the

Graph 4 Mortality Rate for Children Under 5 (deaths per 1,000)

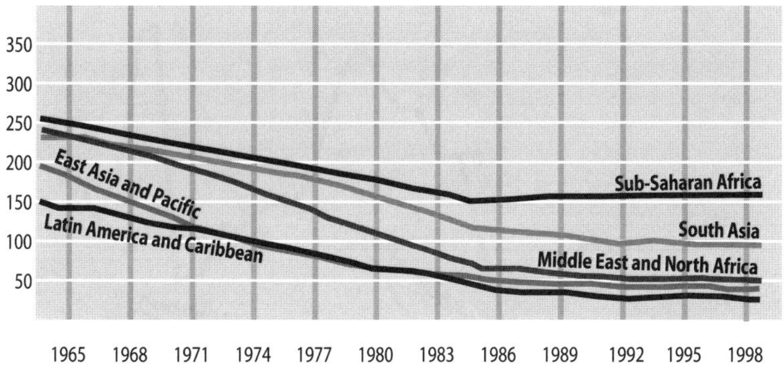

Source: World Bank, *World Development Indicators 2001*.

international community never abandoned Africa; indeed, what is most striking is the willingness of Western countries to keep pouring money into Africa even though it was obvious that it was having little effect. As Nic van de Walle has noted, Africa is already the target of a Marshall Plan. At the height of the original Marshall Plan (after the Second World War), aid accounted for 2.5% of the gross domestic product (GDP) of countries such as France and Germany. In contrast, in 1996, Africa, excluding Nigeria and South Africa received, on average, aid that was the equivalent of 12.3% of GDP.[2] In Mozambique, for example, in 1997, the gross national product (GNP): aid ratio was 43%; in Sao Tomé and Principe 117%; in Guinea-Bissau 71%; and in Rwanda 49%.[3]

It is one of the great disappointments of the post-Second World War era that foreign aid has not produced better results. Certainly, if a domestic policy had a similar record of failure in any industrialised country, it would have been curtailed many years ago. We now understand that foreign aid can be part of a country's development success but only if that country is committed to development (as opposed, say, to using all available resources to promote the political fortunes of its leadership) and if basic governance is good enough to enable the money to be used effectively.

Leaders who are not dedicated to development can divert aid and circumvent the will of donors in countless ways. Donors may demand that their money be used effectively, but, if a country does not have the necessary commitment and governance structures in place, it will be wasted. Of course, many donors have not always prioritised

Graph 5 Aid Per Capita (constant US$)

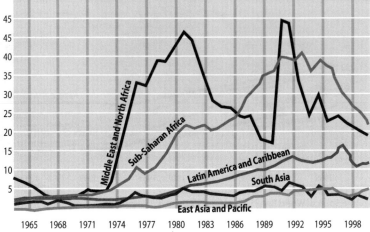

Source: World Bank, *World Development Indicators 2001*.

development. Much foreign aid has been given for strategic reasons and due to historical ties (especially between European countries and their former colonies), rather than because of clear economic assessments of who will use the money best. Conditionalities have varied from being over-extensive to scarcely applied, and nearly always predicated as much on the domestic political needs of the donor as on the longer-term requirements of the target state. The utility of foreign aid is also blunted when Western countries use it to hire their own consultants or to demand that purchases be made from their own suppliers. Past experience and recent commitments in turn raise questions not only about the focus of aid but also about the role and extent of conditionality and the wider relationship between the donor and the recipient nation.

Growing heterogeneity

The second important observation to note when examining Africa is the continent's heterogeneity. When the focus shifts from the regional to the country level, it becomes obvious that Africa's growth record is increasingly varied. Some African countries have become significantly richer and others considerably poorer in the post-independence period. The uneven effect of conflict only served to accentuate differences in growth performance. In particular, some of the countries that have done particularly poorly (Liberia, Sierra Leone and Somalia, for instance) have experienced a decade or more of war and have a government in name only, if that. In contrast, those relatively few states that have done well (Botswana and Mauritius, for example) are increasingly asking questions that are fundamentally different from those that occupy the rest of Africa. Mauritius, for instance, is working to reorient economic activity on the island away from the textile industry and towards information technology, which will put it in a position to become a rich country in the twenty-first century. By contrast, many other African nations would be delighted to have a textile industry or, at this point, to have a profitable raw-material sector.

It is important to note that extrapolation in regard to one or even a group of countries must be carried out with caution, given that the sample may not be representative of an increasingly divergent whole. Neither the occasional success nor dismal failure may mean much on a continent where the contrast between the extremes is becoming ever greater.

Size counts

In fact, when examined closely, it becomes obvious that the third great trend affecting African economic performance is the exceptionally poor performance of large countries, which have suffered from conflicts related to their diverse ethnic composition. While the DRC (50m people), Ethiopia (63m) and Nigeria (124m) together account for 37% of Africa's total population, they have particularly disappointing development records.

Graph 6 GDP Per Capita by Population Grouping (constant 1995 US$)

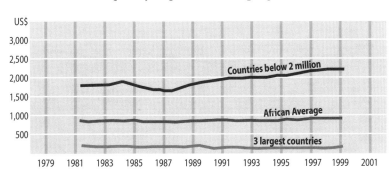

Source: World Bank, *World Bank Africa Database 2002*.

As the chart shows, since 1981 (the first year there is data on Ethiopia), the three African giants have achieved considerably lower rates of per capita income than the African average (their per capita income rates declined by 18% compared to the African average, which increased by 7%). In contrast, the 13 countries with populations below two million[4] enjoyed higher per capita income and grew by 21% between 1981 and 1999. The problem, of course, is that these 13 states account for only 1.7% of Africa's population. Indeed, the fundamental problem affecting Africa is that, overall, the countries that have performed worse than average are those that are extremely large and populous.

When 'average' continental per capita income is calculated, the income of Mauritius ($4,120 per person in 1999, but with a population of only 1.2m) amounts to the same as Ethiopia ($112, but with a population of 63m). The following chart contrasts 'average' continental per capita income with the same figure weighted by population. The latter is essentially what the 'average' African received between 1981 and 1999. As the chart suggests, the experience of the 'average' person is even worse than is suggested by simple continental statistics because the countries with the largest populations have been doing much worse than even the African average.

As a result, one of the underlying problems that African countries appear to face is that of diseconomies of scale. Indeed, it seems more difficult for states to institute good governance procedures in larger countries. The Economic Commission for Africa (ECA) has created an Economic Sustainability Index that aggregates 36 measures of 'sustained growth, human capital development, structural diversification, transaction costs, external dependence, and macro-economic stability'.

Graph 7 GDP Per Capita (constant 1995 US$)

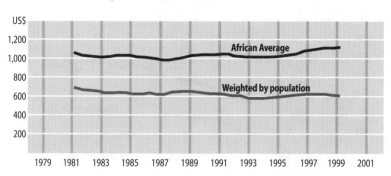

Source: World Bank, *World Bank Africa Database 2002*.

Each country earns a score of between one (low sustainability) and ten (high sustainability).[5] The ECA concludes that: 'The Economic Sustainability Index is uniformly low across the region'.[6]

However, it is interesting to examine the countries that are doing relatively well or badly. The best performers include the Seychelles, Tunisia, Egypt, South Africa, Mauritius, Morocco, Botswana, Lesotho, Swaziland and Algeria. Of those, four are in North Africa. Of the six Sub-Saharan countries, five have populations of less than two million. South Africa is the only one that is not small and that has received a relatively high economic sustainability score. In contrast, the ten worst performers (Sierra Leone, Chad, Niger, Guinea-Bissau, Burundi, the Central African Republic, Uganda, Ethiopia, Mali, and the DRC) include two of the three most populous countries in Africa.

The chronic problem facing the DRC, Ethiopia and Nigeria has been that ethnic divisions have been serious enough to prompt civil war in all three states and, even during peacetime, to force leaders to devote huge resources to patronage in order to try to keep their countries together. Consequently, governance has been especially poor in these three states, which are home to one-third of the population of Sub-Saharan Africa. In addition, Angola and Sudan, two other countries that should have been drivers of African growth because of their size and resource endowments, have instead experienced long periods of conflict. Neither state has been able to exercise authoritative control over large portions of their territory for many years at a time. Hence, while their governments are in no danger of being overthrown, conflict continues to fester in the countryside.

In small countries, meanwhile, there appear to be fewer problems in terms of managing national subdivisions and more resources can be devoted to development. Wars in these states have the potential to end sooner because rebels in the countryside do not find it as difficult to take the battle to the capital and overthrow the government of the day. That is not to say that small size necessarily guarantees development in Sub-Saharan Africa or that no small state experiences long periods of conflict. There are certainly small countries that have been dysfunctional. Given a committed leadership and the right political dynamics, though, smaller nations appear to have some advantages.

Of course, when large countries perform poorly, the aftershocks are felt throughout their respective regions. The DRC, Ethiopia and Nigeria are big enough that, if they did well, the trade demands would promote significant economic activity with their neighbours. Instead, these three countries pose a continual threat to their neighbours because their poor economic record has a dampening effect on the dynamism of their regions. When conflict breaks out in big countries, inevitably, there are spill-over effects, as guns, refugees and crime are exported to neighbouring countries that can do little to insulate themselves from the disaster next door. In the DRC, the instability has also drawn in neighbouring countries, which feel that they must intervene to protect their security, and which are tempted by the opportunity to exploit the Congo's vast mineral wealth. Thus, the question in many parts of Africa has not been so much how to promote regional integration but how to protect countries from the decline of their larger neighbours.

Unfortunately, the international community has not focused on just how poorly Africa's large states are doing. It is instructive to look at Nigeria as an example of the pathologies of large African states because, unlike Congo or Ethiopia, it has not recently been embroiled in a civil war. Nigeria's long-term integrity as a state is increasingly open to doubt. A number of states in the north have adopted Sharia law, indicating contempt for the federal constitution. Obasanjo's government has responded in a distinctly mild manner to this brazen legal challenge.

The Nigerian government is also able to deal with political challenges in the crudest of manners, often using blunt force to silence opponents. For instance, in October 2001, in the central-eastern state of Benue, the Nigerian Army killed more than 200 unarmed civilians in three days. According to Human Rights Watch, the killings were well-planned exercises in collective punishment in response to the deaths of 19 Nigerian soldiers.[7] Obasanjo initially defended the action by his soldiers, intimating that it was to be expected from the military. He later apologised for it. These extra-judicial executions have further exacerbated tensions in a country where ethnic and religious disputes have claimed thousands of lives in recent years.

What is surprising about the massacre is that, except for Human Rights Watch and a few other human-rights campaigners, the event met with silence. UN Secretary-General Kofi Annan has not publicly admonished Nigeria. No Security Council meetings have focused on Nigeria – even though if it were to disintegrate, much of West Africa would be threatened by economic instability and refugee flows. European parliamentarians did not agonise over how to punish Nigeria. And no one has hinted that Obasanjo is a war criminal; rather, he is praised for leading the NEPAD initiative, which seeks to promote governance in Africa.

The truth is that this African giant – with well over 100m people – is slowly disintegrating. Communal violence and open warfare between Nigeria's different communities are now common. The police and the military are both corrupt institutions that are generally helpless to promote order except through the use of extreme violence. The state has atrophied to such a degree that most government ministries can deliver little; the expectations of the population are lower still. Yet, Obasanjo seems more interested in being a global citizen than in tackling the many different challenges that threaten to erode the backbone of his state. It may just be a matter of time before the right spark causes a major breakdown, which will trigger a tremendous humanitarian emergency in Nigeria and, potentially, in the wider West African region.

Assessing Africa's insecurities ...

Africa's security problems are neither recent nor unexpected. Given that it took European countries hundreds of years to evolve into reasonably functioning nation-states, it would be extremely surprising if all were well with countries that have yet to celebrate their fiftieth year of independent rule. The peaceful beginnings of most African states in the 1960s did, however, give a misleading impression of what was in store for the continent. In particular, the fact that the UN was willing to grant sovereignty to many countries that did not control their territories postponed the challenge that many regimes would face in regard to consolidating their rule over large areas where people were often sparsely settled and where there were few roads and little trace of many government institutions. Possession of the capital rather than control of territory appears, in many African cases, to provide sufficient legitimacy for government and for international recognition. By the 1990s, reportedly one-third of Sub-Saharan African states were unable to exercise control over their rural regions, or to extend control to their borders.[8]

It was relatively easy to maintain appearances in the 1960s and 1970s. In most countries, the afterglow associated with the peaceful achievement of power lasted for years. Most African economies were growing, buoyed by global economic growth and relatively high prices for basic commodity exports, which formed the basis of the formal economies of most African countries. The global strategic competition between the Soviet Union and the US also discouraged threats to the design of states in Africa or elsewhere. One of the implicit rules of the Cold War – adopted by the OAU – was that supporting efforts to change frontiers was not part of the game. In fact, the great powers usually intervened (as with Chad, Ethiopia and Zaire) to protect the integrity of existing states.

As a consequence of numerous changes, the real nature of the sovereignty of at least some African countries is being exposed. The economic crisis that many African nations have experienced since the late 1970s has resulted in profound erosion of their national revenue base. Even the most basic agents of the state – such as tax collectors and census-takers – are no longer to be found in many rural areas. Some states are increasingly unable to exercise physical control over their territories. The extremely limited revenue base of many African countries, though, is also partially responsible for one of the most notable developments on the continent in the past 30 years: the change in the military balance between state and society. Whatever their other problems, African states at independence usually controlled the few weapons in their country. As states atrophy, however, their militaries and police agencies also degenerate: readiness declines as there are no funds for training, equipment is no longer maintained, and many soldiers go unpaid. At the same time, those who wish to challenge a government have been able to arm, helped by flow of armaments from conflict zones throughout the region and by the cheap price of weaponry after the Cold War.

Finally, not only is the amount of aid to Africa decreasing from its peak, more critically, donors are redirecting the remaining assistance to countries that are achieving some success with relation to their economic and political reforms. It is only natural, therefore, that those states that are failing spiral further downward. Somalia, for example, was placed on a particularly sharp downward trajectory partly because it could no longer play the US off against the Soviet Union in order to receive more aid. It is precisely those states – including Chad, Ethiopia, Liberia, Sudan and the former Zaire – that received large amounts of aid during the Cold War that have declined the most now that donors no longer reward them simply because of their putative strategic significance.

Given the disappearance of so many domestic and international supports, it was inevitable that some African states would collapse. The contradiction in regard to states with incomplete control over their hinterlands making full claims to sovereignty was too fundamental to remain submerged for long. The turning point came in January 1986, when Yoweri Museveni took power in Uganda. This was the first time that power had been seized in independent Africa by a leader who had gone back to the bush and formed his own army. It was a literal instance of the hinterland striking back. Previous military takeovers had originated in the national army and were essentially palace coups. Soon after, men in other countries who had a taste for power and a grievance with which to mobilise followers found that there was an under-policed and incompletely controlled space in rural areas where they could assemble a rebel force.

Hence, since 1986, armies created to compete against national forces in Chad, Congo (Brazzaville), Ethiopia, Rwanda, Sierra Leone and Zaire have been able to take power by securing outright military victory. Other countries – including the Central African Republic, Guinea–Bissau and Liberia – have experienced dramatic conflicts that have resulted in mass destruction. The wars in Angola and Sudan, lasting decades, have been particularly devastating for hundreds of thousands of people, as rebels in the hinterlands fight capitals in wars that no one can win.

In some countries, state failure has meant that no one has been able to take charge. In Somalia, in January 1991, Siad Barre's government was overthrown but no other group was powerful enough to succeed it – there was a complete collapse of order. At various points in the Liberian civil war, the government's writ did not extend beyond or even within the capital, Monrovia. In such situations, populations have been subject to horrific abuse, as warlords and teenagers with machine-guns terrorise and extort the unarmed.

The failure of states to control their own territories has also greatly increased the dangers of regional conflicts, as countries move to protect their vital interests. The war in the DRC has its origins in the breakdown of the old Zairean state. Rwanda and Uganda initiated the rebellion, which, eventually (in 1997), resulted in Laurent Kabila overthrowing Mobutu Sese Seko. Both countries were under threat from militants who were part of the old Hutu government in Rwanda and who had found sanctuary in eastern Zaire after the Tutsis came to power in 1994. The rebellion was supposed simply to eradicate Hutu militants, but each time the insurgents confronted the Zairean Army, Mobutu's soldiers ran away, partly because they were not willing to fight for a government that had not paid them.

However, Kabila was unwilling or unable to provide the security guarantees that his erstwhile patrons demanded and Kampala and Kigali, therefore, initiated a new insurgency in 1998. This almost succeeded in overthrowing Kabila; Angola, Namibia, and Zimbabwe intervened to keep him in power, to combat Rwanda, and to exploit the Congo's mineral resources. It is obvious that no matter who eventually wins the war, no one will be in control of the vast territory of the DRC for many years to come. Thus, peace, if it sticks, will likely only manifest in pieces.

Several trends are apparent within the complex and shifting African security environment. First, national security apparatuses have been weakened as a result of the international community's decision to terminate military assistance because additional spending on defence is carefully monitored by international organisations, and because domestic financial crises have caused a general weakening of the state. Two agencies have suffered in particular: the police and the intelligence services. Most African police forces are extremely weak and cannot combat day-to-day crime, much less be front-line forces in tackling instability. Intelligence collection is often primitive in African countries. It is very hard for leaders to evaluate changing threat environments; the eruption of armed violence often comes as a surprise to national authorities.

Second, it seems exceedingly easy for rebels to gain access to enough guns and military equipment to be an almost instantly credible threat to many weak governments. In the post-Cold War world, the existence of large numbers of weapons, the continued involvement of former colonial powers (notably France) in African affairs, the emergence of resource wars (mostly over diamonds and oil), the unequal distribution of wealth between urban and rural areas, and the impact of new factors, such as HIV/AIDS, can lead to instability within and between states. Wars that were sustained by external actors during the Cold War continued, partly because they could not simply be turned off, especially in cases where foreign powers had little at stake and where no serious attempt was made to resolve them. Mercenary contracts – often in exchange for diamond and oil leases – also contributed to continued war.

Nascent international efforts to control small arms have, to date, been overwhelmed by traders who now move light weaponry like almost any other commodity. Many African governments (legitimately) fear being outgunned if a rebel movement emerges in their country.

Third, wars in Africa can assume a logic of their own: armies may be less interested in combat than in their own enrichment. Security forces are often so weak that combat is hardly central to the mission of rebel movements. The only reason that the Resistencia Nacional Mocambicana (RENAMO) in Mozambique could operate as such a thuggish organisation (a high percentage of its soldiers were abductees), for example, was because the Frente de Libertacao de Mocambique (FRELIMO) government was so inept.[9] RENAMO acquired a significant amount of its weaponry from fleeing FRELIMO troops. Similarly, given that Somali clans and militias in Congo (Brazzaville) do not face a state, they are able to operate as looting agencies.

One of the central reasons why rebellions that appear to have looting as their primary goal have appeared more frequently in recent years is not because, as David Keen suggests, rebel movements have become weaker,[10] but, rather, because states have become weaker, especially in light of the poor development record described above. While rebellion in Africa was previously against strong settler states, it is now against weak and disintegrating independent governments. Rebel leaders who, like water, choose the path of least resistance can rely increasingly on coercion and looting while not being overly concerned that they will be defeated on the battlefield.

Accordingly, it is no surprise that diseconomies of scale in Africa have fed directly into security problems for larger countries. By definition, large countries have greater trouble policing their territories, especially in Africa, where most of the political and economic infrastructure tends to be concentrated in a capital city. Given that large countries have especially bleak financial prospects, it has been hard for them to ensure security in large parts of their territory. The wars in Angola, the DRC and Sudan dragged on for many years, as neither side was able to win but both the rebels and the government found the means necessary to survive. More generally, with only a few notable exceptions, almost every African country is vulnerable to insecurity in light of the poor development record of recent years.

... and the impact on the West

Inevitably, the implications of Africa's insecurities will not be confined to Africa. Indeed, the events of 11 September 2001 and the bombings in

Bali, Indonesia, on 12 October 2002, underscored the linkage between internal security – graphically portrayed by state collapse, failure to modernise and widespread poverty – and external security concerns. Such connections are emphasised in the 2002 US National Security Strategy.

Former US Assistant Secretary of State for African Affairs Susan Rice said in testimony to the US Congress in November 2001 that: 'Africa is unfortunately the world's soft underbelly for global terrorism'.[11] Such concerns are inevitable perhaps, given that more than one-third of Africa's 800m people are Muslim, and given the ties between Islamic groups and terrorism on the continent. Yet, until recently, it was argued that African Islam could not be radicalised and thus did not pose a fundamentalist threat. Rather, Islam had been 'Africanised' on the continent. This myth has been dispelled, however, by the establishment of Sharia law in 12 of Nigeria's northern states, the branding of Sudan's self-proclaimed Islamic government by the US as a state sponsor of terrorism (having, inter alia, provided a home to Osama bin Laden between 1991 and 1996), and the alleged existence of al-Qaeda cells in Cape Town and the Islamic-linked terrorist attacks in South Africa under the auspices of the Cape Town-based People Against Gangsterism and Drugs (PAGAD).[12] Such fears were heightened by the August 1998 bombings of US embassies in Kenya and Tanzania, which cost more than 200 lives, and the bomb and missile attacks on Israeli tourists in Kenya in late 2002. As Rice has noted: 'the fact that some of Islam's most radical and anti-American adherents are increasingly active from South Africa to Sudan, from Nigeria to Algeria should be of great concern to us'.[13]

It is perhaps not surprising that Islam offers an alternative in this environment. Well-funded by Gulf states (notably Saudi Arabia) after the 1973 oil-price hike, fuelled by lack of delivery and democracy within Africa, and sparked by the apparently unchecked activities of Israel in the Middle East and the export of these troubles to Africa, the continent has been, in Rice's words, a 'veritable incubator' for terrorism and its foot soldiers. The weak nature of the African state and the corruptibility of the African political class have, over time, made it a soft target for terrorist groups. This is complicated, furthermore, by ambiguity about the distinction between a 'terrorist' and a 'freedom fighter' (a consequence of the liberation wars) and latent hostility towards the West over colonial and post-colonial policies.

Paradoxically, Bush administration officials have asserted that Africa, with such a large Muslim population, could play a 'pivotal role' in solidifying support for the War on Terror. US National Security Advisor Condoleezza Rice, in October 2001, urged 'African nations, particularly with large Muslim populations, to speak out at every opportunity to make clear that this is not a war of civilisations, that this is a war of civilisation against those who would be uncivilised in their approach to us'.[14]

Lack of security in Africa allows enemies of states – both in Africa and the West – to operate freely and, therefore, to pose numerous threats to the existing order. Now is thus an especially critical time to examine what policies African and Western nations can agree on to reduce insecurity on the continent.

Chapter 2

Western Responses to Africa's Crisis

Industrialised countries have responded to the economic and security problems that plague Africa. That they remain engaged is, according to some international-relations theorists, surprising. Indeed, if countries were calculators, always determining their actions by how they could incrementally improve their national interest, they would have walked away from Africa a long time ago. The continent's economic and political marginality is such that, in many ways, it does not matter to the industrialised world. Africa's economic product is only 1% of world product and its share of the latter has been in decline for some time.

While approximately one-quarter of the world's sovereign states are located in Africa, many of them are small; indeed, countries south of the Sahara are home only to about 11% of the global population,[1] suggesting that the average African state has significantly fewer people than the average country. The few large countries in Africa in which a disproportionate percentage of the continent's population resides are functioning poorly.

Finally, the economic interests of the West increasingly centre on fossil-fuel investment. US dependency on oil imports from Africa is predicted to increase from 15% today to 25% by 2005. Nigeria is already the fifth-leading foreign supplier of crude oil to the US. However, the platforms that Western companies are building to exploit oil in West and Southern Africa are either offshore or insulated enough from domestic political developments that the oil keeps flowing no matter what happens. Western companies did good business in Angola, for instance, despite the civil war. Undoubtedly, they can get what they want without massive Western political engagement in Africa.

Graph 8 Africa's Share of World Output (percent)

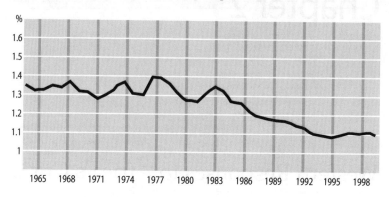

Source: World Bank, *World Bank Development Indicators 2002.*

Some believe that Africa will eventually emerge from its current doldrums and become an important market for the West. Western countries also remain engaged for the opposite reason: the humanitarian tragedy occurring in Sub-Saharan Africa continues to move many people in Western societies. A number of Western leaders appear to be motivated by a mixture of humanitarian and personal concerns, as well as by national interest. UK Prime Minister Tony Blair, for example, has made Africa a focus of his second term of office, arguing at the October 2001 Labour Party Conference that: 'The state of Africa is a scar on the conscience of the world. But if the world as a community focused on it, we could heal it. And if we don't, it will become deeper and angrier'.[2]

As Blair's comments suggest, many in the West believe that, sooner or later, some of the ills that currently afflict Africa will be exported to the West. In particular, there is concern that Africa will be a reservoir for HIV/AIDS, and potentially other diseases. Since 11 September 2001, there has also been concern that those who oppose the West may take advantage of the relative lawlessness in Africa to seek sanctuary and to establish operational bases. Whether this is true or not is unclear, but the issue is serious enough to interest some Western security agencies. The link between terrorism and organised crime, especially in regard to drugs, is another point of concern.

Finally, there are domestic political and bureaucratic considerations. Roughly 13% of the US population traces its ancestry to Africa and African-Americans form a distinct, albeit halting and sometimes unenthusiastic, lobby. This diaspora is constantly changing in composition, but not in importance, reflecting the rapid rate of population increase in Africa and the process of ageing in the West. Africa should represent around 22% of the world's population in 2050 compared to 9% in 1950. Much younger than Europe's population, it is not difficult to imagine a rapid rise in the number of Africans seeking work in the labour-starved economies of the North.

Africa will become too big to ignore; in particular, that African countries constitute a plurality at the UN has an inevitable magnetic effect on Western foreign ministries. Bureaucracies in foreign ministries, aid agencies and intelligence services sometimes wish to remain engaged in Africa because they want to retain their funding, bureaux and mission. Added to these traditional offices is the burgeoning number of non-government organisations (NGOs) that increasingly implement humanitarian policy on behalf of Western governments. These contracts are exceptionally lucrative for NGOs and many, ironically, would not exist without the money they receive from Western governments to operate in Africa. Consequently, they have become a tremendously strong force for Western involvement in Africa. Indeed, it often seems that, especially in Europe, the major NGOs are determining government policy towards Africa.

As a result of this varied constellation of interests, there is a continual schizophrenia in Western countries over whether policy towards Africa should be based on a set of 'goods' (such as a potential market, palpable improvements in some democratic practices over the past decade and rising investment in the natural-resource sector) or on a set of 'bads' (such as HIV/AIDS, war, terrorism, crime and refugee flows). This confusion over motivations has an effect on the rhetoric and substance of Western policy. For instance, Susan Rice, in a speech in Nairobi, Kenya, in November 2002 (essentially her valedictory), painted a picture of two different African futures.[3] It is worth focusing on this oration because the administration of US President Bill Clinton more self-consciously than any other Western country tried to engage Africa in a number of different ways. In accentuating the positive, Rice highlighted the economic achievements of some countries:

> *In the first future, Africa in the year 2020 is alive with possibilities and potential. A growing number of African countries are beginning to build a more secure and*

prosperous foundation for their citizens. These countries are reforming their economies and attracting significant international capital. Growth rates average over six percent annually, and a number of African lions are replicating the economic transformation of parts of Asia and Latin America. Regional markets are increasingly integrated, and their largest members are reaching per capita GDP levels that place them at the doorstep of the community of middle-income states.

The problem, of course, with basing policy on positive developments in Africa is that it requires a large amount of wishful thinking, given current African realities. There is a lot to be done to reach the levels of economic management required, and the political foundations for growth and regional integration.

In the year 2020, over thirty-five African countries fall squarely on the democratic side of the ledger. Nigeria, South Africa, and Kenya are anchors of democracy, assisting their neighbours and serving as compelling examples for the entire continent. The rule of law and strong political parties replace largely personal politics. Responsible legislatures, fair judicial systems, dynamic civil societies, and vibrant and free press are the norm – no longer shackled by repressive leaders. Women are the engine of Africa's progress as they achieve greater prominence and recognition. Women are successful entrepreneurs, civic leaders, and elected officials, including Presidents and Prime Ministers.

Again, this would require a significant change from the current African trajectory. While there has been a laudable evolution from the one-party or no-party regimes that dominated Africa in the 1980s, the number of true democracies (that is, countries whose rulers rotate regularly) is not growing.

Rice, of course, was extremely conscious of the weak reeds on which she based the case for engagement in Africa. Hence, she was careful to enunciate what she called 'Africa's other potential future'. This was a more-or-less classical recitation of Afro-pessimism that would please almost all sceptics:

> *But, Africa's other potential future – twenty years from now*
> *– is far more depressing. The conflicts of the late 1990s have*
> *re-ignited or escalated. Africa's heart – central Africa – is a*
> *region of squandered promise and ongoing exploitation. The*
> *cycle of genocide in the Great Lakes region continues with*
> *impunity. Millions of African civilians are displaced. HIV/*
> *AIDS continues to ravage the continent and lowers the GDP*
> *in most African states by over two percent every year. More*
> *than 120 million children – six times the number of children*
> *now living in the United Kingdom – are orphaned. These*
> *orphans, uneducated and homeless, have fallen prey to all*
> *manner of negative forces. The vast technology gap between*
> *Africa and the rest of the world leaves Africa with no possible*
> *competitive edge, no way to communicate efficiently or to*
> *trade effectively with their European, American, and Asian*
> *partners. Economic growth is negative. Finally, in 2020,*
> *coups like those last year in Guinea-Bissau, Côte d'Ivoire,*
> *Comoros, and Niger are the norm. For most African countries,*
> *democracy remains a distant memory. Africa, in short,*
> *remains mired in poverty, disease, and conflict.*

As is typical in such speeches, Rice assumed that enough Western effort and African goodwill would allow Africa as a whole to seize the option of a positive future. The likelihood that Africa would simply continue to become more heterogeneous – with some (largely small) countries grasping the good future while many (including the continent's big countries) continued to fail – is not something that she chose to contemplate. In fact, most Western officials (undoubtedly including Rice) recognise that the mixed path is by far the most likely scenario. But making the case for engagement on the basis of an increasingly varied continent requires more nuance than most public officials are willing to offer in a public speech. Thus, Western officials almost invariably find themselves exaggerating the case for Africa, either for good or for bad, and seldom inform the publics that they are trying to mobilise about what is actually going to happen in Africa.

Bush's trip to five Sub-Saharan African countries (in order, Senegal, South Africa, Botswana, Uganda, and Nigeria) in July 2003 reflected the trends long apparent in the West's approach to Africa.

Indeed, despite the fact that Africa seemed to be a low priority for Republicans in the 2000 presidential campaign, Bush has been surprisingly attentive to the needs of the continent. The Millennium Challenge Account promises significant new money for Africa and the $15bn HIV/AIDS initiative proposed in the January 2003 State of the Union address and passed by Congress in May should largely benefit Africa. In fact, Bush may be on his way to becoming the US president to be most engaged with Sub-Saharan Africa. His trip was probably just as important to Washington as it was to Botswana or Uganda, since those championing Africa's cause can point to his visit, during the inevitable bureaucratic battles that will occur in the near future, as a clear sign that American engagement with Africa should continue. Once again, Western interest in Africa far surpasses what is suggested by calculations regarding the 'national interest'.

Speaking at Goree Island, Senegal, Bush presented a fascinating synthesis of positive and negative factors:

> *Because Africans and Americans share a belief in the values of liberty and dignity, we must share in the labor of advancing those values. In a time of growing commerce across the globe, we will ensure that the nations of Africa are full partners in the trade and prosperity of the world. Against the waste and violence of civil war, we will stand together for peace. Against the merciless terrorists who threaten every nation, we will wage an unrelenting campaign of justice. Confronted with desperate hunger, we will answer with human compassion and the tools of human technology. In the face of spreading disease, we will join with you in turning the tide against AIDS in Africa.*[4]

While this statement acknowledged Africa's hopes and problems, it tied Africa–US relations more to shared beliefs than to actual interest in solving a particular problem. Of course, relations based on shared beliefs would be plausible if Africa's largest countries were able to demonstrate that they are good examples of the expressed commitment to liberty, dignity and economic advancement.

The endless search for African partners

Wanting to be engaged for non-traditional reasons and without always being able to articulate persuasively why they are engaged has meant that Western countries have often sought proxies. France, the Soviet Union, the US and others, therefore, engaged with dysfunctional leaders in order to advance their strategic interests at little cost. This approach has continued in Africa, even though the competition between the superpowers has ended. Susan Rice, for instance, put out an extraordinary call for African interlocutors:

> *As a new Administration prepares to take office, it is important for Africans to remember that partnership is a two-way street. You have the right to remind us of our shared responsibilities. The United States does not have the option of not dealing with Europe or Asia or Latin America. They are there and we have to take their opportunities and challenges into account. The same holds true for Africa. You are there and we have to engage. African nations must not wait passively to see what the future holds. You should pull up a chair and demand that the US take a chair on the opposite side of the table. That is what true partnership is all about.*

It would be hard to find another region where the US had to look for countries that would sit 'on the opposite side of the table'. India and Mexico, for example, had no doubt that they wanted the US to engage with them.

While the Clinton administration often portrayed itself as the exemplar of Western engagement with Africa, other administrations and countries have the same ambitions when it comes to Africa and face many of the same problems. The Bush administration, for instance, despite its protestations that it is much more realistic than its predecessors and more businesslike in its foreign-policy approach, expresses the same enthusiasm for Africa. In a 2002 speech to business executives, for example, US Secretary of State Colin Powell said:

> *From top to bottom in the Bush Administration we are all committed to doing everything we can to realize Africa's potential. I am asking each and every one of you, in turn and collectively, to bring your enterprise, your know-how, your experience, your capital, to bear on the challenge of helping Africans develop the continent's enormous human and*

> *natural resources. It is an obligation we have. It is part of America's destiny to reach out to people in need, to reach out to all the members of our human family. And nowhere is this more important than in Africa.*[5]

Accordingly, the Bush administration came to power with a fairly explicit agenda to develop ties with a small number of prominent countries in order to engage Africa in a low-cost but effective way. This reasoning underscores, for instance, the US National Security Strategy.

This document pinpoints four states in Africa with which the US should work – Ethiopia, Kenya, Nigeria and South Africa – on the grounds that they have a 'major impact on their neighbourhood' and, as such, 'are anchors for regional engagement and require focused attention'.[6] However, the relatively poor performance of these large countries has meant that it has been exceptionally difficult to advance America's interests. Nigeria's status as a failing state has meant that, inevitably, Washington's partnership with Abuja has been restricted. It should have been relatively easy to work with Pretoria, but the partnership has yielded only limited gains. Nowhere is this clearer than in regard to Zimbabwe, where a South Africa–US partnership to address the catastrophic decline brought about by President Robert Mugabe's regime would have been an important and potentially successful venture. However, South Africa has shown no interest in leading a coalition to confront Mugabe or even, for that matter, in being part of such an alliance.

Instead of being an issue on which South Africa and the US could productively centre their relationship, thereby nipping a failing state in the bud, Zimbabwe has become a thorn in the side of cooperation. Despite his administration's expressed concerns about the deteriorating economic, political and humanitarian situation in Zimbabwe and the continent's failed attempts to find a solution, Bush, on his 2003 trip to Africa, preferred to defer to Mbeki and his efforts to resolve the crisis, referring to him as 'the point man' and an 'honest broker'. This reflects Washington's focus on the War on Terror and on forging a modus vivendi with the South African president and other African leaders in order to concentrate on bigger (global) strategic issues.

The small countries that are succeeding and that have interests aligned with those of the great powers are hardly able to serve as partners. Botswana may have made its distaste for Mugabe public but it is not a nation with which the West can work to confront Zimbabwe. Similarly, the good economic news that has emerged from some of Africa's very small countries cannot be harnessed to sustain Western interests. Thus, while the performance of Botswana and Mauritius is to be applauded, it barely matters in global terms. The fact that oil has been discovered in some of West Africa's small states, including Equatorial Guinea and Sao Tomé, will only exacerbate the disjunction between where the West's very limited economic interests reside and where it may be able to find political partners.

Energetic conservatism

One of the other consequences of Western desire to be engaged in Africa for non-traditional reasons but without a set of natural interlocutors is a policy that paradoxically stresses energy and conservatism. The energy is highlighted in a particular type of engagement rhetoric. For instance, the West has often been content to offer aid as a symbol without demanding results. Typical of Western discourse over aid was a 2002 statement by Baroness Valerie Amos, the then Parliamentary Under-Secretary of State in the UK Foreign and Commonwealth Office:

> *The Prime Minister has made Africa a priority for this government. He underlined this commitment during his visit to West Africa in February. His speech to the Nigerian National Assembly sets this out clearly. In July, we announced the increase of UK Official Development Assistance by £1.5 billion, to reach 0.4 percent of national income by 2005–06. This is the biggest ever rise in UK aid, making a 93 percent real terms increase since 1997. It will include a £1bn annual bilateral programme for Africa. Like the Prime Minister I believe that it is in everyone's interests – both in Africa and more widely – that Africa finds its proper place in the global community. The UK is committed to working to achieve this.*[7]

What is missing from the statement is any notion of what this aid will buy. When governments, businesses or households are serious about something, they feature their goals rather than the means of achieving them. Thus, the Pentagon may state that it is willing to fight two wars simultaneously but it does not say that spending more money is a defence policy. Similarly, a serious foreign aid policy would specify what the West hoped to buy, as opposed to what donors planned to spend. However, stating how much money is going to be spent meets the primary objective of wanting to appear to be engaged without being held to account. The Clinton administration was continually trumpeting the number of fora it had created for dialogue with Africans without ever specifying if all of this talk led to action. For instance, Susan Rice noted:

> *Remaining actively engaged in the new fora we have created will facilitate attaining our goals and objectives in Africa. These fora include the US–South Africa Binational Commission, the US–Nigeria Joint Economic Partnership Commission, the US–Angola Bilateral Consultative Commission, the US-Southern African Development Community Forum, and the US–Africa ministerial, which was the first-ever meeting of African and American ministers. They are critical to our growing partnership with the African people and deserve the next Administration's full support.*

The process was apparently an end in itself with little in the way of results expected.

This conservatism is especially apparent in relation to Western reluctance to contribute to truly new thinking about solutions to Africa's problems. For example, the West has been notably conservative when it comes to the question of sovereignty and the possibility that some nations may have to be redesigned. Western countries have observed, to the letter, the African norm that colonial boundaries are the only legitimate frontiers in Africa, despite the common African complaint that it is the West that is calling the shots. Thus, although the case for Eritrean independence was viewed as legitimate and reasonable (and although Ethiopia was a communist country until 1990), the West was content to observe the African norm that 'breakaway' states should not be recognised.

Nor has the end of the Cold War prompted the West to think more creatively. The Clinton administration devoted extraordinary attention to Sub-Saharan Africa, yet its eagerness to promote stability in Africa was not matched by urgency to develop new approaches to conflict resolution. Rather, it wanted to do more of the same, just with greater energy. Consequently, it failed. With regard to the conflict in the DRC, for example, Rice said: 'In numerous public statements and through energetic diplomatic action we have affirmed our strong and unyielding support for the sovereignty and territorial integrity of the Congo'.[8] This is despite the fact that it is obvious that the DRC has no territorial integrity, has not been an integral unit for many years, and will not be for many more to come. The Bush administration was quick to maintain its predecessor's line. In a 2001 speech to the South African Institute of International Affairs (SAIIA), for instance, Powell said: 'And I want to state very clearly to the people of Congo that the United States will not support any outcome that does not preserve the territorial integrity and sovereignty of Congo. Partition will not bring lasting peace, and we will not support it'.[9]

Similarly, no country recognises the breakaway state of Somaliland, despite the relatively (for Somalia) good performance of the government in Hargeysa and the fact that Somalilanders have a good case for independence (Somaliland was a separate, sovereign state for five days before it merged with the Somali Republic to form Somalia in 1960). The conservatism of the West with regard to the maintenance of boundaries is an especially critical issue because the pathologies of the large countries are inimically connected with their design. Congo fails not only because it has had bad leaders but also because its large size and multi-ethnic composition make it difficult, if not impossible, to rule. Nigeria's continuing failure also derives, in good part, from its inability to address the north–south split, which has been at the heart of the major political problems that it has faced since independence. It may not be the case that the final answer to the problems afflicting the DRC, Nigeria, Sudan and other large African countries is to split them up or otherwise redesign them. Yet, not even to consider the option seems peculiar, especially given how much the West says that it wants to engage with Africa and how determined Western leaders proclaim that they want Africa's future to be different from its past. Western leaders want to show that they care without taking the difficult decisions that may be necessary.

Despite protestations of engagement and the seriousness of the problems, conservatism manifests in the first instance because all bureaucracies hate to change standard operating procedures. Western officials have become accustomed to a landscape that includes the DRC, Nigeria and Sudan and are loathe to initiate a series of events that might cause radical change. The particular type of engagement Western officials have sought with Africa also largely precludes policies that would require expenditure of significant amounts of intellectual and political capital. Western officials have few new ideas for Africa and do not want to develop the analytical structures necessary to instigate dramatic new initiatives. For instance, the Millennium Challenge Account grant announced by Bush in Monterrey, Mexico, on 22 March 2002 earmarked new money for the developing world, but it continued to link progress to economic and governance reforms – the bedrock of most aid agreements over the past 20 years, as well as of the African Growth and Opportunity Act (AGOA). Beyond adding to the kitty and modifying the formula for conditionality available for the developing world, the Bush initiative was notably short on new ideas. Western diplomats are also afraid that proposals pertaining to sovereignty in Africa might resonate in other regions (such as in Russia), where upsetting territorial arrangements might, at least in regard to Western interests, be destabilising.

Overall, the West's approach to Africa presents far more opportunities than is normally suspected, especially by Africans. There is no discernable project that the West somehow seeks to impose on Africa. Rather, the Western posture is one of seeking to be engaged at low cost. In some ways, the scarce resource for the West is not so much money as ideas. It is looking to Africa to provide ideas consonant with now established norms regarding economic reform and governance. Beyond that, though, it is relatively open to initiatives. Indeed, the fact that the West has few strategic interests in Africa means that it might be more open to ideas that challenge fundamental structures. More resources would probably be forthcoming from the West if Africa were to present important ideas that had a reasonable chance of being implemented and of bringing about a reversal in its present depressing trajectory. Here the West's lack of clarity about what it hopes to achieve in Africa is one of the potential strengths of NEPAD. For instance, NEPAD addresses the philosophical question about the role of aid in Africa on behalf of Western states. The challenge, however, is to translate good ideas into development and growth.

But it is clear that the West remains extremely interested in what role South Africa and other pivotal African states can and will play in Africa – as a bridge for the West. This is not a new concept, of course, particularly in relation to South Africa. Afrikaners pictured themselves as having a similar role. The same might be argued for other states, especially given the growing and influential African diaspora in Europe and the US.

Chapter 3

Paradox and Parallax:
The Special Case of South Africa?[1]

South Africa seemingly breaks the mould of the poorly performing big state. Moreover, the country's democratic transition has removed not only the last colonial issue from Africa, enabling, inter alia, the transition from the OAU to the AU, but it has allowed the region to shift the focus away from apartheid and towards its own recovery and development.

In the first decade since the advent of non-racial democracy (in 1994), South Africa has raised constitution-making to new heights, held two successive free, fair and largely peaceful elections and has taken the lead in formulating NEPAD as a comprehensive African recovery programme. To regions of the globe still plagued by secular conflict, South Africa's transition to democracy is exemplary. In this regard, it is apposite that the republic hosted the 2001 World Conference against Racism, Racial Discrimination, Xenophobia and Related Intolerance (WCAR), as well as the World Summit on Sustainable Development (WSSD) in August–September 2002. Even the most hardened Afro-pessimist has been forced grudgingly to acknowledge the profundity of the country's achievements against considerable odds. South Africa presents much that is commendable, particularly when viewed against what might have been.

But much, arguably much more, is expected in Africa from a country that generates 45% and 75%, respectively, of the combined GDP of Sub-Saharan Africa and of the region of the Southern African Development Community (SADC).[2] Pretoria, though, has been reluctant to exercise its continental leadership on crucial issues, such as Zimbabwe, and has increasingly taken a tough foreign-policy line towards some of its key Western partners, notably the UK and the US, over, for example, Iraq and Zimbabwe. And South Africa is also increasingly marked by failure to deliver on a host of core challenges that, collectively, threaten to curtail the consolidation of democracy. Key among them is quixotic political leadership, policy inertia and failure to tackle effectively the congenital maladies embedded as a result of decades of apartheid.

Political parallax and economic delivery?

Since he took over from Nelson Mandela in May 1999, Thabo Mbeki (South Africa's second democratically elected president) has staked a great deal on reforming Africa's relationship with the international system, as a necessary precursor to the continent emerging from decades of poverty and political chaos. In doing so, he has cut an impressive, if at times controversial, figure on the global stage. His pragmatism, visible in the manner in which he has, for example, taken Africa's case (in the form of NEPAD) to the G8, contrasts with his eccentric claim that there is not a link between HIV and AIDS, which affects one in nine of his own people and 25m Africans across the continent. However, the apparently positive reception that Mbeki received from Western leadership stands in contrast to his relations with some domestic constituencies, notably over racial reconciliation. There are also tensions within his own ruling African National Congress (ANC) and in regard to its alliance with the Congress of South African Trade Unions (COSATU) and the South African Communist Party (SACP). Much of this relates to the pace of economic delivery in South Africa, and to the centralisation of power under Mbeki.[3]

The South African economy stands out in Africa not only in terms of its size, but also in terms of depth of expertise, technology and management.[4] Macroeconomic fundamentals and their management remain sound. Fiscal policy is robust, the deficit having fallen from 9% in 1993 to 1.4% by 2002. Monetary policy is healthy, with the introduction of inflation targeting, an increasingly strong (and liberalised) exchange rate and a reduction in the government's forward open-book position from $4.8bn in 2001 to $1.5bn in 2003. The government has committed to trade liberalisation partly through the signing of a number of agreements establishing free-trade areas, including that with the European Union (EU), with the average tariff falling from 15.1% in 1997 to 6.5% by 2001.[5] Combined with the existence of a vigorous and highly regulated financial sector, this has resulted in improvements in South Africa's credit ratings since 2000.

Yet there are still significant hurdles to overcome in order to meet the high post-apartheid expectations of South Africa's population. Unemployment stands at around 35%, with a net job loss since 1994 of more than 500,000. The lower-than-expected rate of inward FDI[6] reflects the slow pace of privatisation, high if falling levels of criminality, concerns about the cost and volatility of labour and low levels of expertise, and fears about intrusive government policy to legislate black economic empowerment. Crucially, it also reflects concerns about the deteriorating security situation in Zimbabwe, and how Mbeki has handled it.

Indeed, Mbeki's attempts to sell Africa as a development package through NEPAD have been criticised because of the slow pace of delivery in South Africa, and, paradoxically, because of the need to separate South Africa in the eyes of the investor community from the rest of Africa. Conversely, while many black South Africans respond to the region's challenges and migration movements (towards South Africa) in increasingly xenophobic ways, Southern Africans have themselves a jaundiced yet hopeful view of the role that the continent's giant might play.

South Africa's foreign policy: a bridge for the West in Africa?

As mentioned earlier, the 2002 US National Security Strategy pinpoints four partner African states with which the US should work: Ethiopia, Kenya, Nigeria and South Africa.[7] But how willing are these states to act in concert with Western interests, not only in their respective regions, but further afield? And to what extent will unwillingness to partner Washington and other major allies globally affect the nature of Western support for wider foreign-policy ambitions, notably NEPAD?

South Africa is the key state in this process. It is expected to lead, but its reliability and effectiveness as a partner of the West is in question. This relates both to its history and to its worldview.

For example, Mandela's criticism of US-led diplomatic action towards Iraq is one clear illustration of South Africa's *Weltanschauung*. At the December 2002 ANC conference in Cape Town, he attacked US foreign policy, saying that the country's approach to Iraq was arrogant and demonstrated alarming indifference towards the UN. Arguing that '[w]e cannot allow a superpower to disregard the UN', he said that world peace could be achieved only if all nations, including the most powerful, adhered to its founding principles. Mandela believed that the behaviour of the US and the UK towards Iraq not only violated those principles but that it was also 'dangerously' close to neglecting the concept of multilateralism.[8] He later accused the US of being racist and of having 'a president who can't think properly', and claimed that Bush wanted to plunge the world into a 'holocaust'.[9]

Mandela is, however, not alone in holding such views among South Africa's ruling elite. In January 2003, Mbeki lambasted those who threatened Iraq with war but did nothing about Israel's nuclear weapons, saying 'the matter has nothing to do with principle … it turns solely on the question of power [and] we disagree'.[10] A day after Mbeki insisted that his government was not anti-American, ANC Secretary-General Kgalema Motlanthe told some 4,000 anti-war demonstrators outside the US Embassy in Pretoria that South Africa, with its rich mineral resources, could be the next target of US action 'if we don't stop this unilateral action against Iraq today'.[11] Earlier, following Powell's presentation to the UN Security Council in February 2003, Smuts Ngonyama, the head of the presidency in the ANC, dismissed the evidence against Iraq as 'fabrication'.[12] In December 2002, when asked by Britain's *The Guardian* newspaper if the necessary funding for anti-retroviral drugs could come from money earmarked for the submarines that form part of a multi-billion arms deal, South African Health Minister Manto Tshabalala-Msimang reportedly said that the country needed to deter aggressors: 'Look at what Bush is doing … [h]e could invade'.[13]

In November 2002, South African Deputy Foreign Minister Aziz Pahad paid a visit to Baghdad where he met with President Saddam Hussein. The intention was reportedly to impress upon Saddam the need to comply with all UN Security Council resolutions. Yet Pretoria's position was informed, as Pahad admitted, by what it saw as the dangers of the US policy of 'regime change', which 'would explode the entire region'.[14] Mbeki defended Pahad's meeting with Saddam on the grounds that the US was aware of, and 'pleased' with South Africa's engagement with Iraq.[15] In February 2003, Pretoria controversially sent a mission of disarmament experts to Iraq to try to prevent war.

Nevertheless, South Africa and the US share many interests, and hence there is a lot at stake. They enjoy a burgeoning bilateral trade and investment relationship. The US has been the largest investor in South

Africa since 1994, with investments amounting to more than $2.5bn by the end of the decade. During the 1990s, bilateral trade grew by more than $2bn, with over $6bn in two-way business by 2000. Growth has been especially rapid in manufacturing goods and services. A South Africa–US free-trade area is now on the cards. Put differently, the US is a key partner if NEPAD is to achieve its ambitious goals.

South Africa's international foreign-policy stance contradicts strongly with the pragmatism that its government has displayed at home, not only with regard to racial reconciliation, but also, especially, in relation to its pursuit of conservative macroeconomic policies. The emphasis on reducing inflation and controlling expenditure is surprising from a party that is social democratic if not socialist in ideological origin. And it is all the more surprising from a party elected by South Africa's poorest classes, which were long denied equal economic access and brought up on a political diet that explained their plight in terms of the excesses of Western capitalism.

Yet, understanding the twists and turns in South African foreign-policy requires knowledge of the background of the ANC and its ruling elite.

In 1993, a year before assuming office, Mandela stated that: 'Human rights will be the light that guides our foreign affairs'.[16] During his presidency (1994–99), South Africa's foreign relations were dominated both by his iconic personality and by the country's bid for re-acceptance in the community of nations. As Mandela gathered international plaudits, Pretoria expanded its bilateral ties to more than 90 overseas missions. South Africa took its seat in a variety of international fora, including the UN General Assembly, the 14-member SADC, the Commonwealth and the Non-Aligned Movement (NAM). Under Mbeki, it has gone on to chair the Commonwealth and the NAM. The hosting, in quick succession, of the World AIDS Conference in 2000, the WCAR in 2001, and, in 2002, both the inaugural meeting of the AU (in July) and the WSSD (in August–September), has reinforced its global prominence. But its strongly independent line on Iraq and Zimbabwe has increasingly come to the fore as South Africa's international position has normalised. Underlying this is anti-Western sentiment, not informed by direct interests, but rather by a history of colonisation and apartheid and the socialist background of many members of the ANC leadership, as well as by historical ambivalence and, indeed, the outright opposition of some Western leaders, notably Margaret Thatcher and Ronald Reagan, to the ANC. This contrasts with the support received from the NAM and socialist-bloc countries. It is also shaped, in the case of the Middle East, by religion; and, more importantly, overall, by a vociferous Muslim minority. Certainly, race and anti-colonialism have determined the ANC's policy towards Zimbabwe, where many see South Africa's 'quiet diplomacy' as little more than an excuse for inaction. While Pretoria has presented the alternatives as being between talking to Harare and invasion,[17] this is not the reality, although it does speak volumes about the constraints under which the ANC operates at home and regionally. Electorates largely support Mugabe's action on the grounds that it has dispossessed white farmers and cocked a snook at Britain. In spite of the impact of Mugabe's misrule on mainly black Zimbabweans, Mbeki's administration has consistently referred to the Zimbabwe crisis in terms of land distribution; the solution consequently resting with the UK's refusal to pay for more resettlement. Pretoria will not, in the circumstances, act against Mugabe. As Foreign Minister Nkosazana Dlamini-Zuma put it in March 2003: condemnation of Harare's actions 'will never happen so long as this [ANC] government is in power'.[18]

During a visit to Zimbabwe in late 2002, Dlamini-Zuma stated that she had not seen any sign of bloodshed. At the ANC's 2002 conference in Stellenbosch, furthermore, she hailed Mugabe's Zimbabwe African National Union-Patriotic Front (ZANU-PF) as a 'progressive party'. At the same conference, Mbeki noted: 'We are … convinced that it is necessary to bring to a close the controversial issues relating to our important neighbour, Zimbabwe … In this regard, we are ready to engage both our ally and fellow liberation movement, ZANU-PF, and all others concerned to help resolve the various issues in a constructive manner'.[19]

This may also indicate, to a degree, Pretoria's unease with the rise of the union-based opposition Movement for Democratic Change in Zimbabwe, and the related failure of ZANU-PF to change fully from a liberation movement to a political party. Similar challenges could confront the ANC, a party whose regional reputation and role reflect partly the military ineffectiveness with which it prosecuted the liberation cause in South Africa, and partly the high cost to South Africa's neighbours of offering support for that struggle. As one senior party member put it in January 2003: 'The ANC does not command the respect of the Mugabes in the region precisely because, unlike them, it did not shoot its way to power'.

Central to differences in perception over Zimbabwe between South Africa and its key NEPAD partners is Mbeki's focus on the need for a global power shift. In this light, NEPAD is not just about improving the economic lot of Africans through good governance and adherence to the rule of law, but also it is about changing the nature of the relationship between the North and the South – between Africa and its political and economic colonisers – which he believes is at the root of this inequality. According to this view, there can be no long-term sustainable transformation and development in Africa without reform of the UN and the global trade and financial architecture. This, one analyst has noted, 'is the objective that drives all [of Mbeki's] policy initiatives'.[20] As the president has argued:[21]

> *"Unipolarity" and "unilateralism" mean that one power, with a little help from its friends, takes decisions about what happens in the world, including our countries, without our participation. This represents an undemocratic "new" world order that turns us, once more, into "the invisible people of the world", living in fear of the consequences of responding to our consciences, because of our dependence on the wealthy and developed world. "Multilateralism" and an effective United Nations mean that we would have the possibility to contribute to the solution of the problems facing humanity, including ourselves. This would mark the emergence of a new world order, characterised by the democratisation of the system of international relations and the availability of the space for the poor and powerless freely to speak their minds, in a world that is being integrated and made more interdependent by the unstoppable process of globalisation.*

He continued:

> *The processes relating to the question of Iraq confirm the disturbing reality that unilateralism, rather than multi-lateralism, has become the dominant tendency in world politics. They confirm the painful truth that economic, military, technological and other power constitutes the political engine that determines the fate of all humanity.*

The danger is, however, that Mbeki is biting off more than he can chew, and that he is simultaneously risking South Africa's hard-won moral high-ground, both in Africa and beyond. His stance over Iraq does not square with Pretoria's quiet diplomacy over Zimbabwe. While Pretoria was prepared to devote time and considerable resources to settling the Iraq situation peacefully, the same commitment has not been made publicly to solving Zimbabwe's crisis. It not only neglects the rapidly worsening socio-economic and political situation in Zimbabwe, but also risks fallout with South Africa's SADC partners. In comparison, Botswanan President Festus Mogae has described the situation as follows: 'It is a drought of good governance that is much more difficult because you have neighbours like Zimbabwe'.[22]

There is little doubt that much of the ANC's rhetoric is intended for the domestic audience, especially South Africa's Muslim community, which, although it makes up just 2% of the country's 42m-strong population, is politically influential and vocal, especially in regard to Iraq and other matters in which South Africa has sought involvement, such as the Arab–Israeli conflict. There is also a constant need for Pretoria to dismiss the perception of those in Africa that it operates, economically and politically, as little more than an embassy for Western views on the continent. Pretoria thus has to engage in a difficult balancing act, keeping close enough to the US to have a voice, but independent enough to maintain its credentials in Africa and in the South.

But this should not understate the more deeply held views within the ANC about the West in general, and the US and the Republicans in particular. This sentiment is dangerous both to American and South African longer-term interests and to the future of NEPAD. It is as misinformed about the realities of US domestic and foreign policy as it is founded on a combination of perceptions about race, domination, exclusion and imperialism. To this extent, Pretoria remains a costly prisoner of its paradigm of international engagement. It is, therefore, unlikely that South Africa and other states will be allies of the West, but rather, at best, tentative partners of the West in Africa, a complication that will make finding common ground on NEPAD much more difficult.

Chapter 4

NEPAD and the AU: Towards a New Order?

The new international environment presents a tremendous opportunity for Africans if leaders on the continent can propose new initiatives. On the positive side, the grand policy debates of the 1980s – when there was long discussion about the need to devalue overvalued currencies, reform poorly working state enterprises, pay workers market prices, control inflation and decrease deficits – are largely over. For the most part, Africans have rejected the statist economies that they inherited from the colonialists then enhanced, while, to varying degrees, clinging to various socialist doctrines. There is now also consensus across the continent that, while macroeconomic reform is necessary, it will only have the desired effect if it is grounded in good governance. Finally, populations and elites have largely rejected the one- or no-party regimes of the past. This has produced results. Some African economies are beginning to grow again; the continent grew faster than any other region in 2001. Also, many polities are freer than before and there is strong rhetorical commitment to good governance.

Yet, while it is clear that the vast majority of African countries and their leaders are no longer interested in the economic and political policies that brought about stagnation in their economies and polities, they are uncertain about how to adopt the new approaches. There is elite consensus in regard to macroeconomic reforms, but these measures are not popular. Steps to improve governance are popular, but these extremely taxing administrative initiatives can only be adopted slowly given the institutional weaknesses of almost all African states. Finally, although African countries have moved toward multi-party electoral competition, many old autocrats have managed to rig the systems in their favour and many once promising political experiments (such as in Madagascar and Zambia) have all but collapsed. Africans, therefore, are set to embark on a new order of their making. What will it look like?

NEPAD in detail

NEPAD is based on five core initiatives that recognise many of Africa's most important challenges:[1]

- **The Peace, Security, Democracy and Political Governance Initiative** aims to end conflict and to encourage effective, fair, democratic political systems that deliver good governance and respect for human rights.
- **The Economic and Corporate Governance Initiative** aims to strengthen Africa's management of its macroeconomic environment, government budgeting, central-bank operations and corporate governance. It recognises that Africa will depend on private-sector-led growth for poverty alleviation and national improvement.
- **The Capital Flows Initiative** aims to channel greater resources to Africa by encouraging investment, greater debt relief and reform, as well as increased official development assistance.
- **The Market Access Initiative** aims to open foreign markets to African goods and to diversify African production into higher value trade.
- **The Human Resources Initiative** focuses on the critical issues of poverty reduction, education, skills and health.

The most important point to note is that NEPAD must be actively supported and owned by African leaders. The plan states that the continent must create mechanisms to share best practices and to promote standards of good governance and democracy. It also envisions interventions to bring nations into line with NEPAD commitments, although each participating state will design its own plan to conform with NEPAD's objectives. Supported by a permanent secretariat, acting largely in a coordinating function, these plans will be the basis for an African Peer Review Mechanism (APRM), the most innovative dimension of NEPAD.

Less than a fortnight after the 2002 G8's Kananaskis summit, African states convened in Durban, South Africa, to terminate the 30-year-old OAU and to celebrate the advent of the AU, the envisaged vehicle for continental union and, most importantly, the delivery of NEPAD's good-governance and structural programmes. But there has been both overlap and tensions within and between NEPAD and the AU, notably over the mandate and location of the APRM. Some of these problems are inevitable, given the ambitious nature of NEPAD and the AU, especially in terms of changes in domestic and international governance. However, there remain some points of contention due to African leaders' desire to retain as many of their prerogatives as possible, while claiming that Africa will now enforce conditions that had previously been the responsibility of the international financial institutions. Whether these are the labour pains of a new order or signs of chronic stress that will be the doom of both initiatives is the critical next question for Africa's leaders.

First, NEPAD essentially argues that, unless there is a new aid and governance regime, African states will not be able to achieve the growth rates that will lift them above their current levels of incapacity and poverty. This argument suggests that, without a special environment, African states will not be able to succeed – that is, they are essentially uncompetitive, even dysfunctional entities. But is NEPAD sufficient to remedy this condition? Does the call for a new regime imply a re-examination of core problems with the African state? Put simply, African states are generally weak, fragmented and arbitrarily defined units, where African leadership has conveniently used the OAU moratorium (reiterated in the AU's founding document) to perpetuate colonial borders and poor government. In particular, is NEPAD capable of dealing with the problems of large states whose poor performance has been such a striking feature of African development over the past 20 years? African countries may have been given the correct diagnosis but is the medicine they have prescribed – basically the same measures as before but with a stronger local flavour – sufficient to treat it? It appears that the obstacles are daunting.

Second, as noted above, African governments, under NEPAD, will commit themselves to standards of good governance and democracy through a system of peer review and institutional mechanisms. These are the foundations for the operation of the programme, the core principles of successful development without which donors will be loathe to invest at current, let alone increased levels. Yet, while the mechanisms for review are clear enough on paper, they are reliant on considerable institutional capacity and the sort of political will that, hitherto, has been lacking among African governments. Again, the fact that it is the large African countries – the ones with presumably the most influence – that, on average, are the worst performing makes this an especially difficult task. How can Nigeria, for instance, act as a peer reviewer of its neighbours' governance policies when its own have been dysfunctional for so long?

This tension is manifest in the debate about which process – NEPAD or the AU – would take responsibility for peer review, the critical factor in setting and maintaining African governance standards. As one commentator has noted: 'NEPAD exists in an ambiguous zone'.[2] It stands for better governance, but it is an AU programme, vulnerable to the many agendas of its members, as well as to undermining as a result of the expansion of its core implementation group, via the inclusion of such countries as Kenya and Libya with questionable democratic credentials. But these states are powerful and influential, with Libya reportedly likely to pay the membership dues of one-third of the AU's membership, as it did with the OAU.

The distinction and relationship between the AU and NEPAD with regard to peer review and, in turn, their linkage with other bodies, such as the Conference on Security, Stability, Development and Co-operation in Africa (CSSDCA) – created by Obasanjo in 1991 – is unclear. The picture is further complicated by the role of key institutions within the peer-review process: the NEPAD Secretariat, the AU Commission, and the UN's ECA have all sought a role. Ahead of the fifth NEPAD implementation committee meeting in Abuja, Nigeria, in November 2002, the South African government cast doubt on whether the APRM would examine both economic/corporate and political governance, with the AU now being deemed responsible for political review through its own structures.

This confusion created a stir, because the G8 and others had understood that NEPAD (and peer review) would include a common commitment to democracy, rule of law, openness, human rights, and so on.[3] The lack of clarity, costly to NEPAD's external image as a new African developmental regime, also arguably reflected both misunderstanding of the original intention to integrate the programme within the AU and the degree of resistance encountered from various

African governments (notably Nigeria, which favoured the CSSDCA as NEPAD's coordinating mechanism) to removing political review from the APRM secretariat.[4]

Finally, the different expectations reflect the democratic realities within African states, where democracy is often only barely entrenched and scarcely understood. Liberalisation is anathema to the majority of

Table 1	Political Rights and Civil Liberties		
	Free	Partly Free	Not Free
Freest economies	Botswana		
Less free	Benin Cape Verde Ghana Mali Mauritius Namibia South Africa	Burkina Faso Central African Republic Côte d'Ivoire Ethiopia Gabon Gambia Lesotho Madagascar Mauritania Mozambique Niger Senegal Tanzania Uganda Zambia	Cameron Chad Guinea Kenya Swaziland
Excessively regulated		Congo-Brazzaville Guinea-Bissau Malawi Nigeria Sierra Leone Togo	Equatorial Guinea Rwanda Zimbabwe

Not ranked		Comoros
		Seychelles
			Angola
			Burundi
			Democratic
			  Republic of
			  Congo
			Eritrea
			Liberia
			Somalia
			Sudan

African states. The table (on page 53) displays the current state of reform in Africa, using Freedom House's rankings for political rights and civil liberties and the Heritage Foundation's Index of Economic Freedom.[5]

Cross-referencing produces a very short list of African states with economic and political freedoms that rank in the free category for political rights and civil liberties and that also have done a fairly good job in deregulating their economies. This highlights less a concern about the efficacy, applicability and sequencing of market reforms within democratic political systems, than it reflects the extraordinary difficulties that Africa's NEPAD proponents face in selling a liberalising economic and political roadmap to vulnerable African leadership.

Ironically, the creation of NEPAD and the AU underlined the lack of democracy in most African states. In most countries, there was little to no discussion of the plan to improve democracy and governance across the continent. There was more debate between leaders behind closed doors over the shape of the plan than there was in any one country. Nor did any African leader actually try to convince his polity that accepting peer review by fellow African countries was a positive move. This was particularly ironic given the record of African criticism of conditionality, as practised by the international financial institutions, which failed to respect the sovereign and democratic prerogatives of borrowing countries.

To an extent, NEPAD is hostage to progress within the AU; and the latter reflects many of the failings of its predecessor. As Kingsley Mamabolo, South African Deputy Director-General (Africa) in the Department of Foreign Affairs, has commented: 'The AU is clearly a very ambitious project with 18 organs with wings and arms and so on to be established. Right now we are inheriting the OAU's liabilities as well as its assets, including back dues of US$42 million'.[6] Mbeki has correspondingly sought to allay fears that the AU's role in peer review would weaken Africa's resolve to uphold democratic practices. Following the November 2002 Abuja meeting, he stated that: 'it is critically important to understand that this review system contains both voluntary and obligatory categories ... Matters of political governance among the member states of the AU are governed by such instruments as the Constitutive Act of the African Union ... As with any law, its observance is obligatory and not voluntary. In reality the Constitutive Act is an African treaty that binds all member states of the AU to its provisions'.[7] But the OAU's history of sovereign non-interference and collegiality rather than rigorous application of principle and standards, has left many doubting the effectiveness of the peer-review process and thus the new beginning apparently offered by NEPAD. Only time will tell whether Africa is sincere about the advent of a new, stricter regime informed by democracy and good governance. Given the failures of the past, though, the burden of proof is clearly on the Africans.

Third, NEPAD assumes to some degree that aid works, although the evidence of the past 30 years is that it does not work in cases where capacity and good policy are absent. Yet, African states now want more aid, with fewer external conditions attached, when the evidence is not that conditionality per se failed, but that the regimes and institutions applying it failed in their application and weakened their resolve. This issue, in turn, raises questions about how external actions can create or supplant internal capacity.

Fourth, business and civil society have provided little input to the process. The logic of business underscores the need to conduct thorough risk-and-return analysis before making any (particularly long-term) fixed investment. Thus, business requires structured channels within NEPAD to articulate its interests. The role of business is crucial, not least because the bulk of the $64bn targeted for annual investment has to come from this sector. There remains a danger that business, the engine of growth, and government see NEPAD in different terms: the former primarily in terms of the creation of conditions in which business can prosper – the rule of law, free markets and good governance; the latter in terms of increased aid and developmental projects. They have been talking past each other in this regard, with NEPAD seen by many as a compact between African leaders, not between leaders and their people.

Finally, NEPAD places great store on regional units functioning effectively, although the evidence from Africa in this regard is patchy. Problems of under-capacity, lack of political will, and a relative absence of economic complementarity have blighted such attempts, from the Union of Arab Maghreb (UMA) in North Africa, through the Economic Community of West African States (ECOWAS), the East African Community (EAC), and the Common Market for Eastern and Southern Africa (COMESA), to the SADC.

A key question for NEPAD, therefore, is how should one measure progress? In this respect, there is a need to make a critical distinction between proof of process and of delivery.

In terms of coordination, the small NEPAD Secretariat has achieved remarkable success in the 18 months of its existence. Based in the offices of the Development Bank of Southern Africa (DBSA) in Midrand, South Africa, the Secretariat, at the start of 2003, comprised seconded officials from the five initiating states: Algeria, Egypt, Nigeria, Senegal and South Africa. It is charged with providing logistical support and programme facilitation. Despite myriad continental challenges (and challengers), coordinating mechanisms have been set up that seek to streamline political, trade and commercial linkages and to avoid unnecessary duplication, particularly among the regional economic communities. Furthermore, the South African government has established a model for inter-departmental coordination on NEPAD. Government ministries have appointed dedicated officials, while NEPAD also now features in the business plans of South African diplomatic missions. An outreach programme has been created to provide points of entry for NGOs, while a number of NEPAD business chapters are, at least in principle, now functional.

Externally, coordination is occurring at eight different levels:

- First, with the Heads of State (so-called Lusaka) Implementation Committee. Comprising three countries per region (with a fourth to be appointed), this body sets policy parameters and identifies priorities. Ultimately, it reports to the AU summit.
- Second, with the Steering Committee. This body meets monthly and consists of personal representatives of the heads of state along with a number of seconded officials from the AU and the African Development Bank (ADB). Its focus is on developing programmes of action.
- Third, with the AU and the CSSDCA. Although the exact role of the Nigerian-promoted CSSDCA is yet to be determined, there is a need, given its focus on peer review, to avoid potential overlap with the embryonic APRM.
- Fourth, with the seven recognised regional economic communities. The objective is to ensure that so-called Regional Indicative Strategic Development Plans (RISDPs) are consistent with NEPAD's goals.
- Fifth, with other relevant inter-governmental African organisations, including the African Capacity-Building Organ (ACBO), the ECA and the ADB, especially given the mooted role of the

latter two organisations in economic and corporate governance under the APRM.

- Sixth, with member states. The aim is to link NEPAD with national development strategies and to enable outreach within these countries.
- Seventh, with the international system, involving a plethora of bodies, such as the Bretton Woods institutions, the Commonwealth, the EU, the G8, the NAM, the Nordic states, the Organisation for Economic Co-operation and Development (OECD), the Sino-Africa Forum and the UN and its agencies.
- Eighth, with civil society and business, encompassing, for instance, the African Development Forum, the African Scholars Forum, the Organisation of African Trade Unions and the institutions of the AU, including the Pan-African Parliament. Aside from the continental domain, there is also a need to promote internal discussion, given that, thus far, just three African countries have held parliamentary debates on NEPAD. Several states have been selected for a pilot outreach project.[8] In addition, a NEPAD Business Group has been formed, involving, inter alia, the Corporate Council on Africa, the Commonwealth Business Forum and the International Chamber of Commerce.

While the establishment of coordinating mechanisms lays the foundations for the achievement of NEPAD's goals, it is not an end in itself. Improved coordination per se cannot deliver essential new investment or projects to the continent. Furthermore, planning and coordinating activities have not tangibly altered the investment climate in Africa. Nor are such activities marketable to the international investment community. While re-branding commercial projects (such as those emanating from South African-based parastatals) as NEPAD deliverables is one short-term way around this, in the longer-term, there needs to be a clear set of projects that would not have come about without NEPAD.

The need for roll-out and momentum

It is true, therefore, that NEPAD and the AU face a multitude of challenges, not least in dealing with the extreme differences between African states, which range from fully-fledged liberal democracies and export-oriented, high-tech economies (such as South Africa) to military dictatorships with highly-centralised, command-style economic systems. These differences were graphically illustrated at Durban in July 2002 by Libyan President Muammar Gaddafi's attempts to hijack the AU for his own political ends. Gaddafi wanted to alter the AU's Constitutive Act to ensure that he wrested control of the AU Commission away from its inaugural chair, South Africa, and host the African parliament – in spite of the fact that Libya can hardly be considered a democracy.

Other challenges exist in terms of servicing the plethora of AU institutions, which include:

- the aforementioned African parliament (nominated from five African regions – Central, East, North, South and West Africa) and the commission (a permanent secretariat modelled on the European Commission, operating out of the AU's headquarters);
- an Assembly, comprising all heads of state, and serving as the supreme decision-making body;
- an Executive Council, made up of ministers of foreign affairs;
- the Permanent Representatives Committee, composed of AU country representatives;
- various specialised technical committees, dealing with the rural economy, finance and monetary matters, science and technology, transport and communications, health, labour and social affairs, trade and immigration, and education and culture;
- the Court of Justice, focusing on human-rights issues;
- the UN Economic and Social Council (ECOSOC), an advisory body composed of professional and civic representatives;
- financial institutions, including an African Central Bank, the African Monetary Fund and the African Investment Bank;
- the Peace and Security Council, a 15-member entity tasked with monitoring and intervening in conflicts.

The differences between the South African AU hosts and the preferences of Gaddafi reflect wider political and economic differences across the continent: between the reformers – those in Africa willing and able to carry out the sort of structural reforms demanded – and the recalcitrants – those unwilling or unable to consent to the types of measures suggested by NEPAD and the cession of sovereign control implicit in the AU's constitution. Already, African leaders, suspicious of South African leadership and fearful of African – rather than World Bank – or IMF-imposed conditionalities and invasive peer review, have sought privately to undermine NEPAD's dictates as 'yet another

Structural Adjustment Programme', a kiss of policy death in an African context. These differences and the need to sustain continent-wide support were manifest in the agreement made at the fourth NEPAD implementation committee meeting in Durban to extend the committee's membership from 15 to 20 states, including, it is mooted, Kenya and Libya.[9]

Grand visions, such as NEPAD and the AU, will require early successes to ensure their credibility among donors and African states alike. The response of the G8 in Kananaskis was lukewarm – at least when measured against African expectations. While there was definite progress on quotas and duty-free access to markets in the North, no new money was forthcoming (save for the earmarking of $5bn at Monterey) and there was no visible progress on eliminating agricultural and other subsidies. Critical to the external community's response to Africa's plan is progress in not only establishing but implementing and sanctioning the peer-review mechanism: as the G8 communiqué put it, peer review 'will inform our considerations of eligibility for enhanced partnerships'.[10]

Regional integration and insecurity

A critical assumption of the African-proposed continental architecture is regional integration. There are obvious benefits flowing from improved regional coordination and cooperation, not least the ending of conflict, the creation of larger, more attractive markets through the removal of barriers to trade and investment, increased investment flows, and the development of much-needed infrastructure. There remain, however, significant obstacles to this process in Africa, especially absent a congruence of democratic and economic values within regions. In particular, the larger African states (such as Congo, Nigeria, Ethiopia and Sudan) have, as noted earlier, done very badly in their respective regions. Rather than acting as engines of growth and sources of stability, these states have been sources of insecurity and economic problems for their neighbours. They have also not provided the leadership solutions that Africa demands.

Another major challenge for African regional integration is simply that, whereas in Europe this process has been the outcome of the development of similar national systems, in Africa, the integration ideal has been used to drive the process. Put crudely, it has been a case of putting the cart before the horse. Lack of a regional transport infrastructure – in most areas significantly degraded from the time of colonialism – is another barrier to greater trade flows and integration. Yet efforts to improve existing rail networks have fallen foul of the interests of ruling elites, including stalled attempts to rehabilitate links between Djibouti and Ethiopia. They have also been subject to the influence of donor agencies.

Arguments in favour of closer integration should thus not obscure the immense challenges facing regional units, as they strive to overcome political differences and economic insecurities. In Africa, region-building has been a difficult task: intra-regional trade accounted, on average, for just 6% of African trade in 1990, and grew to just 10% by the end of the decade. In the case of the SADC region, for example, South Africa's market domination, coupled with differences in leadership style and respect for democratic values and human rights, has made the regional project complex and problematic. Similar difficulties have, unfortunately, been replicated throughout Africa – although, conversely, these arguably make regionalism all the more necessary.

The relatively small size of African markets and their occasionally isolated and inaccessible location undoubtedly constitute problems for regional integration schemes, especially given the large and disparate number of states involved. For example, ECOWAS has 15 members,[11] COMESA 20,[12] and SADC 14. This weakness is exacerbated by duplication of objectives and overlap in terms of membership.

It should be acknowledged that there are often sound political reasons for what appears to be over-rapid regional expansion. Most notable is the need for political inclusivity and dialogue in regions that, in the recent past, have experienced (and in some cases continue to suffer from) conflict and instability. These problems of divergence might (and arguably should) be addressed through the application of variable membership criteria to encourage the incremental centrifugal development of similar economic ideologies and trajectories among member states. These would also take into account their heterogeneous nature.

Indeed, Africa's regional organisations – like those, for example, in Asia during the 1980s and 1990s – have immense value in providing a framework for managing the differences between member states. But this is something that they have largely failed to embrace. Regional differences – due in part to apartheid, the colonial legacy of development, and personality and policy disagreements today – are deep and clearly need to be managed. There does not have to be a contradiction between seeking excellence, deepening integration and providing such a framework, or, put differently, between moving the region forward at a pace that globalisation demands, and not at one that the slowest, most recalcitrant member is prepared to allow.

The answer to the conundrum (between political solidarity and economic convergence) lies, in part, in doing the easy things first with those who want to participate. Encouraging regional variable geometry – by which some states integrate faster than others – is essential to the successful implementation of NEPAD. Many SADC member states are, for instance, radically different in economic and political terms. Some are practising democracies, some clearly not. Some have exchange-rate controls and pegged currencies, some state-controlled banking institutions. And while some have single-digit inflation, others are in triple figures. Failure to adopt a differentiated approach also illustrates why the gains of African states are too often overlooked in sweeping external reviews of the continent.

Any effective regional development strategy must go beyond the general and concentrate on the specific. There has to be a focus on the creation of cheaper and more effective communications and networks, and development of an integrated trade and investment market. The knowledge and skills that drive modern economies must be improved – to which end a massive investment in education is required. Private-sector expertise and resources should also be harnessed and tapped to assist in the development of skills. A regional strategy needs to concentrate especially on those issues that governments and business in partnership can do something about, both at home and regionally.

In terms of settling regional conflicts, NEPAD appears to be paying off. The signature of peace agreements in July 2002 between Kigali and Kinshasa, and between arch-opponents Khartoum and the Sudan People's Liberation Movement/Army (SPLM/A) has resulted in tangible, if bumpy, progress in line with NEPAD's objectives of ensuring stability, security and prosperity. Of course, peace is a process not an agreement. Longer-term stability is dependent on a number of factors, including willingness to engage in continued dialogue and compromise long after the negotiators have departed. This requires, at the most basic level, a stake in the peace, internally and regionally, which is enabled by an inclusive political process. In the case of the DRC, the involvement of the Rwandan-backed Rally for Congolese Democracy (RCD) in a transitional government of national unity will depend on the provision of fundamental security guarantees to Rwanda, its policies still, understandably, determined principally by the genocide of 1994. In Sudan, peace hinges on acceptance of the result of the process of self-determination for the south, however it turns out, and the building of trust between Khartoum and the SPLA, a relationship scarred by 30 years of war.

Importantly, these deals were an outcome of the type of partnership promoted by NEPAD. The Congo–Rwanda agreement was primarily the result of the efforts of the South African negotiating team headed by Deputy President Jacob Zuma. However, it also reflected the role of other actors, including the former UK Secretary of State for International Development Clare Short, and the Blair government on which Kigali is heavily dependent for financial support. Former Kenyan President Daniel Arap Moi chaired the Sudanese peace process – under the auspices of the Inter-Governmental Authority for Development (IGAD) – but its success has depended thus far on the backing of Washington and, importantly, the security guarantees being provided for and by Uganda.

Business and government

Another partnership critical to NEPAD is that between business and government. In Africa (and, indeed, in most developing nations) this relationship is criticised on various grounds, ranging from being too close (with the associated problems of corruption, nepotism and lack of distinction between private and public accounts) and too distant. It is clear that business has a major part to play in the future success (or not) of Africa. Without the commercial sector, there will not be enough jobs, and there will be little in the way of an economy for government to manage or to derive benefit from. Economic conditions impact profoundly on culture, ideology and politics and vice versa. Taking a leaf from Singapore, South Korea and Taiwan, the necessary components of successful reform include the need for a skilled workforce, a policy environment conducive to investment, including political stability, high savings from which to generate local investment, and a developed infrastructure. Africa's inability to generate sufficient investment – local or foreign – has been compounded by the export of financial and human capital.

For business to flourish, however, it requires a favourable environment, particularly in regard to activities like mining, which are, by definition, long-term, high cost endeavours. This affects not only on the role of government in terms of improving the overall economic environment, but also the relationship between government and existing enterprises. Rather than steadfastly urging government to accommodate its demands, business has too often swayed, run scared or at least been reluctant to 'take on' the executive, reflecting the excesses of African rule, lack of legal recourse, and the patrimonial ties between sectors of business and government. At times, furthermore, this has led to seeming acceptance of some of the most odious regimes in Africa.

There is also a need for corporate governance, as distinct from good governance, a fundamental whose importance has been recently highlighted, not only by the corruption that has blighted development in emerging markets, but also by the tribulations of Enron and Worldcom. Corporate governance is not solely a domestic concern: the link between money laundering, transnational threats and poor corporate governance is one that has been underscored by the events of 11 September.

Thus, for business to prosper in Africa, a number of things have to be put right. Among them are: implementation of corporate governance standards, including the timely provision of information to investors; clear separation of interests by executives; strongly enforced independent audit practices; and clear lines of responsibility for corporate leaders.[13] Corporate transparency has wider political benefits too. It forces greater openness in government dealings through disclosure. In most environments, companies are reluctant to divulge information, given the potential risks to their relationship with government and the possible loss of strategic business advantage. Avoiding such practices, though, will raise the cost of doing business in the long term.

There is a leading role to be played by multinational corporations in setting standards for government and local businesses. In the case of Angola, transparency in relation to the activities of oil companies will arguably do more to 'reconnect' Angola's people with its government, deepen democracy and deliver good governance than any form of external aid conditionality. To enable this, multinational corporations have to be encouraged to adopt these practices. Universal standards have to be set. Applying the ethical norms embodied in the AGOA currently being applied to African states – transparency, accountability, disclosure and rule of law – to US and other international companies at home, would be a good starting point. Such leadership would advance economic well-being and security in Africa and among its OECD partners. This should not, however, obscure the need for good governance. NEPAD's success and the success of business in Africa will not hinge on good corporate governance alone, but on the need fundamentally to encourage policy-making regimes that are logical, transparent and not subject to narrow political interests.

Chapter 5

Tasks for the Future

Given the problems of ingrained poverty and state weakness in Africa, NEPAD proposes a special development plan for the continent. In proposing this agenda, African states essentially make a key admission: there is little alternative to IMF/World Bank wisdom in terms of macroeconomic reform and management, despite years of African- and NGO-led criticism of this orthodoxy.

It is clear that command economies in Africa do not work; Angola, Ethiopia, Mozambique and Tanzania provide evidence of this. There is little alternative to liberalisation. Moreover, liberalisation can release and generate scarce capital and broaden the base of wealth in Africa. Governance reforms, too, a precursor to greater onshore investment, provide for increased accountability and thus investor security. That the record of such reforms has been mixed requires a deeper examination of whether they were in fact imposed, how they were implemented, and the role of the political and economic elite.

The difference with NEPAD is that, critically, structural conditionalities are imposed and instigated by Africans – a point that has not gone unnoticed by NEPAD's ideological opponents. However, NEPAD, unlike the Bretton Woods institutions, does not have the financial clout to compel adherence to its conditions. Furthermore, the focus on special developmental conditions for Africa may be an admission of the dysfunctional nature of these states, necessitating huge aid transfers and special external preferences. This poses additional questions about these states' ability to prosper without external assistance and about the relationship between such assistance and the creation of internal governance capacity – in essence, about the long-term efficacy of aid as a development tool.

That, on average, African states are poorer today than at independence prompts a re-examination of both aid policies, on the one hand, and the construct of African states on the other. It raises the core question: what is the formula for African regeneration and success?

The aid Africa needs

Additional aid is a vital feature of NEPAD. Canada has launched a $500m NEPAD fund, while the Bush administration has committed an extra $5bn annually to aid development under the Millennium Challenge Account, much of which will go to Africa.[1] New aid strategies are connected to new debt-relief programmes. Under the IMF/World Bank's Heavily Indebted Poor Countries (HIPC) initiative, 22 African states could, upon acceptance of Poverty Reduction Strategy Papers (PRSPs), receive $33bn of relief, permitting further spending on education and other social services.[2]

The returns on aid have been consistently disappointing. One study found that, in 1990, $1bn in aid lifted 105,000 people above the absolute poverty line of $1 per day. By 1997, the same amount had helped another 284,000 people out of poverty. Put differently, when measured in terms of lifting people from absolute poverty, in 1990, $9,523 (or $3,521 in 1997) was spent in order to lift each beneficiary by $365 per year. As Ross Herbert has argued: 'Given that success rate, would it not be more efficient and effective just to fly planes over Africa and push money out of the doors?'[3] And, although the World Bank claims that the success rate of its projects increased from 60% in the late 1980s to 80% in 2002, much of the analysis was conducted by its Operations Evaluation Department. As Adam Lerrick has put it: 'when the auditors are captive, when the timing of the judgement is premature, when the criteria are faulty and when the numbers are selectively chosen – how credible are the conclusions?'[4] Assessments of other aid programmes, such as those of the EU, have also been questioned.[5]

Indeed, aid has not only failed in empirical terms, but also in regard to its distortion of the relationship between government and the governed. For example, aid flows can result in those with entrepreneurial skills moving from the productive sphere to the aid 'sectors' of the economy, where the opportunities are greater (and where payment is made in hard currency). Aid is also accused of serving as a cushion, enabling Africa to postpone, hijack or avoid reforms that market forces should have made it undertake years before. In this way, aid is seen to work as a powerful disincentive to reform. Although the relationship between donors and recipient nations tends to be a turbulent on–off, love–hate affair, with continuous reassessments of conditions and renegotiation of goals, donor incentives to give or lend money would appear ultimately to outweigh any failure to meet the original terms. There are also questions about the value of the HIPC initiative. Critics have queried, for instance, the imposition of additional conditionalities on countries that have no, or little, record of past adherence to the provisions of structural adjustment programmes.

Research suggests that aid works – or at least works better – when good, reasonable policies are in place. According to the World Bank, aid has helped in Africa when the policy environment has been 'good' or receptive. One Bank report, published in 2001, *Aid and Reform in Africa: Lessons from Ten Case Studies,*[6] found that the quantity of aid that countries received has 'no effect on the quality of their macro-economic policies'.[7] A number of reasons are suggested for this, including the political context, especially the health of the democratic system, and the length of the incumbent government's tenure. Growth rates reflect the success of reforms. Many of the better reformers were those countries that had few options and were mired in crisis. In those judged to be mixed reformers, backsliding occurred as reforms became tougher and politically more intrusive (and expensive). Poor reformers, meanwhile, tend to 'block' the process and the policy changes required.

But which comes first, aid or good policies? And how can the latter be achieved? What is the synergy between making aid more effective, and improving national governance? Essentially, it means imposing the very kinds of structural adjustment programmes that were lambasted by recipient nations as intrusive and destructive during the 1990s. Indeed, the great opportunity for NEPAD is finally to have the aid spent correctly, after decades in which the agendas of both African countries and donors prevented the money from doing much good.

In practice, World Bank theories notwithstanding, the first step for many African nations is thus to work out how to use aid better, especially given high levels of dependence on this source of national income. Instead of simply taking aid, it would be much more constructive to establish what projects could add value to GDP. A second move would be to work out where national comparative advantage lies. Third, it is necessary to recognise the past failure of conditionality, both due to lack of capacity in the target state, and lack of political will in donor and recipient countries. Fewer conditions, more strictly applied, can only help. A fourth critical area is to establish what the private sector, local and foreign, wants in terms of the policy environment, which would attract investment. Whereas a great deal of time and effort is spent on African regional integration (for good political and infrastructural reasons, if nothing else), far less time is spent on understanding and accessing the global market. This is most surprising given that this is a case of a $350bn versus a $30,000bn market.

The trade Africa needs: what the West can do for Africa

Volumes of aid are, therefore, not the problem in African development. Yet, it is clear that the international community will have to come to the party if Africa is to realise rates of growth sufficient to achieve political stability through economic prosperity. In particular, there is a need to reward performing and reforming states in order to provide a normative – if not institutional – global political economy in the longer term. The best way to do this has to be through improved trade access.

According to Mike Moore, if developed countries drop domestic agricultural subsidies, developing states stand to earn at least three times more in exports than they currently receive in international aid. Or, as Belgium Prime Minster Guy Verhofstadt has argued, 'If all world markets were fully opened up to competition, the total income of developing countries would be boosted by US$700 billion per year or 14 times the total development aid that they currently receive'.[8] Allowing developing countries to export agricultural goods to Western nations that currently subsidise their farmers is the quickest way to increase employment and reduce poverty in Africa. Moore has contended that:

> *If we removed those agricultural subsidies, that would return maybe three to five times more than all the overseas development assistance put together. This would return eight times more than all the debt relief ... So the [anti-globalisation] protesters should be protesting about agricultural subsidies not just about debt relief.*[9]

A major advantage for Africa is that its markets are small enough to accommodate preferential access. But such access has to be both conditional and closely monitored, and focused on value-added trade and on reducing, ultimately, non-tariff measures. The AGOA may offer a useful template for future engagement in this regard. By mid-2002, US officials estimated that the AGOA had created an additional 60,000 jobs in Africa, increasing African exports to the US by more than 1,000% and generating nearly $1bn in investment.[10] This could rise even more dramatically now that Bush has signed AGOA II into law.

The EU has taken a different line through development of its Regional Economic Partnership Arrangements (REPAs). Nevertheless, it is similarly focused on trying to improve domestic economic activity as a necessary precursor to taking advantage of preferential trade access.

The role that the international community can play is in opening up trade markets and reducing subsidies, thereby encouraging market reforms and competitiveness – if this is their goal. It has been estimated that a new global trade round could lift 320m people out of poverty; such a process would be five times more effective than providing aid.[11] The success of the AGOA in Africa shows that, given the right (fair) conditions, African manufacturing industries can compete in the global market. Trade openness is crucial, allowing Africa's agricultural sector to play a central role in development. Instability and poor agricultural methods, combined with restrictive trade practices, have meant that, despite the fact that, today, Africa has just half the share of the global agricultural markets since 1980, the number of starving Africans has doubled. Developed countries' agricultural policies represent a tax on African agriculture of up to $7.1bn per annum – or 85% of 2001 bilateral aid flows to the continent. Food and agricultural raw materials account for 27% of African exports today, with the sector employing between 65% and 80% of African workers.[12]

Enabling African countries to compete globally, of course, does not only involve demand-side adjustments, but also improved competitiveness among suppliers. This points to the need to reduce transaction costs, improve infrastructure and to market African goods. Fundamentally, however, Africa's ability to sell goods, particularly manufactured items, abroad, depends on consumer confidence; this, in turn, reflects price, reliability of supply, quality and 'uniqueness' in a hyper-competitive global environment. Reliability of supply and economic transaction costs relate intrinsically to the need to restore African stability.

The security Africa needs: what Africa can do for itself

Each African country that is mired in conflict is different in its own way. At one level, the conflicts that Africa is experiencing have shocked the world in terms of their brutality and pointlessness. At another level, Africa's wars simply reflect the difficulty of creating recognised national authorities that exercise physical control over their territories. Much needs to be done in Africa to end the fighting: Africans must assume greater ownership; the international community must be pro-active in attempting to avert violence; and more has to be done to promote development and to limit the supply of weapons. That is not to say that the way forward is clear, but that individual African states, the AU, and the international community all have a role to play.

There has been less focus, though, on making Africa's security agencies work, so that conflicts can be prevented or ended. Indeed, it is ironic that, just as Africa and the world have focused more on the problems related to conflict on the continent, the notion of victory and defeat has been lost. The Lords Resistance Army in Uganda, the Revolutionary United Front (RUF) in Sierra Leone, and many other rebel/bandit movements in Africa simply need to be defeated. Yet, countless NGOs and mediators do not want to advocate victory, only that the law of war is followed in its pursuit. While there is clearly not a military solution to every problem, it is also not possible to believe that there is a diplomatic answer to all conflicts. Indeed, the current optimism in Angola springs from the Movimento Popular da Libertacao de Angola (MPLA)'s military defeat of UNITA and its seeming resolve to take sensible political steps now that it has triumphed on the battlefield. The international community will have to recognise that victory is an option in some conflicts and work to aid national authorities in winning, instead of just hoping that they fight according to the rules.

The international community has spent more than two decades trying to ensure that Africa's economic institutions function well, but only recently has it focused on promoting the viability of Africa's security institutions (especially the military and the police), even though peace is the prerequisite for economic growth. The fact that countries with large territories face particularly grave problems in regard to national integration is a clear sign that more has to be done to promote the daily provision of security in Africa. Aiding police forces, in particular, so that they can fight crime, deter criminals, and be viable 'first responders' to those who might eventually threaten war is critical. Yet, the international community is only now taking the first steps towards helping police forces in Africa. More has to be done so that African countries that are potentially viable will be able to regulate their territories. The international community will have to become less averse to working with the police, a sensitivity that developed in the 1960s and 1970s after well-publicised scandals, especially in Latin America, and recognise that focusing on development, while simply assuming that security will take care of itself, is a careless strategy.

Yet post-Cold War external intervention in African conflicts has, in the past, been largely guided by a reactive philosophy, with a focus on peacekeeping, for example, rather than preventive diplomacy. This is changing. Peace-building along with conflict resolution has become vogue, although this raises questions, too, about the lessons from past negotiation experiences and the conditions necessary for sustained peace, stability and prosperity. These include the need for a focus on:

- a coherent, inter-disciplinary, tailored multinational approach, whether this be for peace support or for conflict resolution. Peace cannot be brokered where there is disagreement among regional and international partners with the effect that actors can play sides off against each other. Such are the lessons, for instance, from the transition from apartheid in South Africa;
- timing, the building of confidence through second-track diplomacy, and multinational engagement (such as with Zimbabwe);
- creating conditions at the local level so that people can live their lives. Importantly, this stresses the need for peace-building strategies;
- the role of external conditions – even sanctions – in promoting reform and compromise; and
- supporting key aspects of governance, including military reform.

But revitalising state agencies and cementing peace demands that, fundamentally, Africa has the states that it needs.

The states Africa needs

The termination of the OAU was the most dramatic example to date of the radical rethinking that is occurring in Africa regarding the political and economic arrangements inherited from colonialists. As noted above, Africans are also asking key questions about almost every aspect of their polities. Perhaps the most notable issue that has not received enough attention, though, is whether Africa has the states that it needs to develop.

Although NEPAD is to rely on voluntary 'peer review' as a basis for ensuring adherence to good governance norms, its success hinges on the creation of conditions of peace and security. And the need for a new, more interventionist approach is apparent in the AU's Constitutive Act, its apparent intolerance of unconstitutional changes of African government and its call for the creation of an African military standby force. Article 4(h) of the AU's Constitutive Act provides for 'the right to intervene in a Member State pursuant to a decision of the Assembly in respect of grave circumstances, namely: war crimes, genocide and crimes against humanity'. Article 4(j) provides for 'the right of Member States to request intervention from the Union in order to restore peace and security'. And Article 23(2) provides that 'any Member State that fails to comply with the decisions and policies of the Union may be subjected to other sanctions, such as the denial of transport and communications links with other Member States, and other measures of a political and economic nature to be determined by the Assembly'.[13] Indeed, Mbeki has noted that the political and economic integration of Africa raises questions about the sovereignty of states: '[B]ecause we share a common destiny and need all of us to succeed ... national sovereignty should be impacted on by the things that we do ... [and] ... in the process of implementing the integration of the African continent that this matter of boundaries will arise'.[14] Sovereignty may no longer afford protection to abusive governments and leadership. Instead, the debate has shifted to focus on the means to ensure compliance with international norms and the protection of citizens in the face of leadership excesses.

The question of what the alternatives might be to some of Africa's existing dysfunctional states is being explored elsewhere.[15] However, it is striking to note that African reform, as conceptualised by Africans and the international community, essentially stops at the frontier. Every aspect of a country's political economy can be questioned, as long as it is assumed that it will continue to exist. Human history, in contrast, suggests that states capable of promoting development and mass participation in politics emerge slowly over time, usually only after many failures. For instance, the vast majority of attempts to establish states in Europe from 1500 onwards met with failure.[16] European states are durable today because a succession of wars reconfigured their boundaries. One of the great questions for the AU and NEPAD is whether the necessary results can be achieved without changing frontiers.

No one policy will solve the problem that, in parts of Africa, the actual territory states control is far less than what the map suggests. However, it is possible to imagine some real alternatives to the status quo, which would at least be a start in creating political units that correspond to the way power is exercised in Africa. Critically, the question no longer centres on whether all boundaries should be respected. As the tragedy in Central Africa shows, African states are already reacting to state failure by developing their own solutions to their neighbours' failures. But these ad-hoc solutions to the failings of the continental state system will inevitably be extremely problematic. For instance, tiny Rwanda's answer to the crisis in Central Africa was, at the end of the twentieth century, to extend its internal order – dominated by Tutsis – within the region. To avoid such disastrous attempts at self-help, African states and the international community must, pro-actively, develop new policies that recognise the reality of power in Africa or else be doomed to witness ever-greater human tragedy.

The first step in addressing conflict would be to acknowledge that, in some parts of Africa, boundaries themselves are part of the problem and to stop pretending that every African country has been, is, and will always be in full control of its territory. Thus, for the international community to play a constructive role in promoting peace in the DRC, it will be necessary to tear up the old rulebook. The international community should say, plainly and simply, that the DRC is not a sovereign state.

More importantly, challenging the notion that the DRC should be a sovereign entity forever no matter what is happening on the ground opens up the possibility of more interesting diplomatic manoeuvres, which might contribute to ending the fighting permanently. Given that there is no hope of Kinshasa issuing a credible promise to protect Rwanda's and Uganda's interests in eastern DRC (it may not have the physical capacity to do so even if it wanted to), some kind of security zone in eastern DRC might be established. This zone, which might be similar to that which Israel created in southern Lebanon, would allow Rwanda and Uganda to defend their interests, especially by deterring attacks by Hutu elements of the old Rwandan Army, within proscribed DRC territory, perhaps under international supervision. Alternatively, the contested areas of the DRC could gain internationalised status that would allow Rwandan and Ugandan concerns to be met.

Once some of the issues in eastern DRC have been addressed, attention could shift to the fundamental matter of providing regional and international security guarantees to the Tutsi, which might involve deep-seated changes in the nature, and perhaps in the shape of Burundi and Rwanda. This is an enormously complex issue with no obvious resolution. But, unless there is a regional solution to the problem of Tutsi insecurity, forces intervening across borders will probably upset any national solution that is attempted. At least to say that the current map of Central Africa cannot be held constant if there is to be some long-term answer to the Tutsi problem would constitute a refreshing bit of candour.

Beyond Central Africa, it is vital that the international community move away from the notion that once a state achieves membership of the UN General Assembly, it is forever sovereign, no matter what happens within its frontiers. Such a departure from the unthinking acceptances of past diplomatic practices would provide a strong signal that something fundamental has gone wrong in an African country and that elements of the international community are no longer willing to perpetuate the myth that every state is always exercising sovereign authority.

It is increasingly recognised across the continent that the political problems affecting an increasing number of countries will not be solved unless the underlying issue of control of territory is addressed. South of the Sahara there is a growing, although still inchoate, willingness to consider alternatives in the face of catastrophe. Especially after the Rwanda genocide of 1994, many in Africa now realise that alternatives to existing boundaries should at least be considered.

Furthermore, in areas far from the capital, other actors, including traditional leaders and local warlords who have moved into the vacuum created by the collapse of local branches of the state, may exercise substantial control, provide security, and collect taxes. Understanding that, in some of Africa's failed or failing states, rural communities already face a complex situation where sovereign control is exercised only partially, if at all, by the central government would be an important return to reality. In turn, the willingness of the international community to acknowledge that some African states rule less than the territory contained within their boundaries would be a powerful lever when negotiating with African leaders. African presidents, like Joseph Kabila in the DRC, currently benefit from the assumption that they control all of their territory. If sovereignty is no longer assumed, these leaders would be forced, for the first time, to ponder profound changes in the way that they govern (for example, by providing autonomy to some areas, constructing complex power-sharing arrangements to avoid wars, and by making new efforts to construct a national identity) in order to convince the international community that they rule over their territory. Without this lever, there is little reason, given current international practices, for many African leaders to contemplate serious reforms that might put an end to conflict. They are often better off personally remaining as head of a sovereign state, even if their country is at war, than entering into what will inevitably be an uncertain power-sharing arrangement during peacetime. Erasing the assumption that every African state, no matter how problematic, will retain its territorial integrity forever at least opens up the possibility of changing the incentives that led to war in the first place.

The leadership Africa needs

Africans have long demanded African solutions to African problems. They now have their chance. Arguably, for the first time, Africans hold the initiative in the policy debate over how development and security should be promoted. They are shaping the agenda not because their ideas are so compelling but because the performance of so many others has been disappointing and because the West is tired of being criticised for foisting its ideas on the continent. Africa, therefore, needs realism not idealism. Its leaders need to be realistic about the opportunities that NEPAD offers, especially in light of extremely uneven continental performance. Greater realism about the value of aid and the importance of viable security institutions is also required of Africans and of members of the international community. Clearly, the principal attribute separating Africa's performing states from its post-colonial failures is the presence of visionary yet practically inclined leaders, such as Botswana's Sir Seretse Khama, Nelson Mandela or, of a younger generation, Ghana's John Kufuor and Joaquim Chissano of Mozambique. Of course, there are many more examples of poor leadership.

It is intriguing that Africa's leaders have seldom displayed the same type of commitment as their Asian counterparts – Asian leaders, for all their faults, have made the betterment of their people their desired legacy. Perhaps this is because African leadership has experienced such a difficult process of inheritance, possibly because it was natural that the stereotype of colonial authority should be replaced by the African 'big man' dependent on patronage and pomp. African leaders must not avoid the reality that, while they can rail about the injustices of the international order, the only possibility of significantly improving the condition of their people lies in adopting fundamental domestic reforms. If those reforms are not made, there is every reason to believe that the number of failed states in Africa will increase. Those countries that do grasp the fundamental challenges facing them will find at least a mildly supportive international environment. Indeed, NEPAD may improve this environment but it will ultimately fail if the Africans believe that NEPAD is somehow a replacement for making difficult decisions about domestic structures.

Conclusion

Zeitgeist and Realism

NEPAD is as attractive to the West as it is to Africans. For the West, it offers a new possibility to secure African stability – in cases where traditional approaches have failed miserably; for African states and leaders it offers the chance to take responsibility for doing so. If successful, it will present economic opportunities in previously hostile and risky markets, and significantly reduce the threat of a transnational spillover of people and problems arising from African conflicts and failing economies.

For Africans, NEPAD is attractive partly because it offers a more positive future, and partly because it is about Africans developing their own policy precepts, based on their needs and formulated by their leadership. Its success will, to a great extent, depend on the right conditions for international partnership, the right leadership, and recognition by Africans of the importance of differentiation between African states in formulating the right policies for recovery.

The reasons, as detailed in this paper, behind Africa's economic collapse are complex and varied, but include widespread conflict (and the inability of African governments to solve it), failure to consolidate democratic practices, the nature of the colonial inheritance and post-colonial relationships, and, notably, Africa's failure to globalise. The latter is the result of a number of inherited, structural problems with African economies: their initially close linkages with their respective colonial metropole, and their over-focus on aid and trade regimes, which has deepened dependency and institutionalised inefficiencies, rather than spurred greater engagement with the global economy. Although aid efficiency has improved, real per capita income in Africa did not move upwards in spite of huge development assistance. Aid might work better in good policy environments, but the reality is that these are few and far between in Africa.

This reality should not, however, deny the need for closer partnership. There are a range of strategic interests drawing together Europe and the US on the one hand, and Africa's key states – including Egypt, Kenya, Nigeria and South Africa – on the other, particularly on a continent defined more often by the extreme of state collapse than by, for example, the representation by South Africa of a modern, industrialised economy. The focus of the US National Security Strategy on the connection between state collapse and transnational threats should assist Africa in its search for solutions. Such interests are compounded by the shared history of human rights and race, and by contemporary mutual concerns, such as the radicalisation of Islam on the continent. These shared interests are given expression by a burgeoning bilateral trade and investment relationship, strengthened through the establishment of trade preferences under the AGOA and the EU's Cotonou arrangement.

But what are the forms that such partnership might take? One possibility is greater cooperation in multilateral fora, including the Commonwealth, the EU and the UN. However, this will most likely occur only after decisive regional leadership is shown in addressing crises. Thus much is pinned on NEPAD. But NEPAD may only flatter to deceive, due to lack of support within Africa and if external interest weakens.

As one senior Pretoria-based diplomat noted in January 2003: 'At the time of its launch, the zeitgeist for NEPAD was all right'. In a world gripped by the polarising forces of terrorism and war, the zeitgeist for NEPAD is, comparatively, all wrong. Consequently, the African recovery plan is unwisely being shunted down the global order. The war in Iraq and the War on Terror present real and present dangers to NEPAD, particularly if hard earned momentum is lost. What is needed, therefore, is a united and intensified campaign by African leaders to convey the message that NEPAD is good for global security.

In addition to the capital- and attention-draining implications of war and post-conflict reconstruction in the Gulf, NEPAD faces a second, and possibly more debilitating threat: non-delivery. Ironically, though, NEPAD's political leaders appear to be more exercised by the exogenous threat. Indeed, while Africans had little impact on US policy toward Saddam's regime, they are largely masters of their own destiny with regard to converting NEPAD from a blueprint into a programme of action and delivery.

How should Africans go about ensuring that the continent's recovery programme remains on the agenda of the top table? For NEPAD to achieve its objectives will necessitate targeted public–private partnerships. The next phase of its activities should fall increasingly outside the control of politicians, diplomats and bureaucrats and increasingly into the sphere of business executives, investors, engineers, entrepreneurs and, indeed, civil society. This will require that NEPAD's political leadership become listeners more than prescribers, and facilitators rather than implementers. Politicians and bureaucrats do not create wealth, but they can and must create conditions in which, for Africa, the investment zeitgeist is right.

More fundamentally, NEPAD has to be sold to Africans. It is widely perceived as being an elite-driven, exclusive, gender and class insensitive, neo-liberal construct that is not a partnership, but, rather, a collusive programme driven primarily by South Africa with the political support of the UK and the financial support of Canada. It has largely excluded parliamentarians, civil society, trade unions, think-tanks and the media. By January 2003, for example, only three parliaments had held formal debates on NEPAD. African trade-union federations have rejected it in its current form, while churches and academics have been highly critical. Leadership in Africa, and particularly in its leading state, South Africa, has been strong on symbolism, rhetoric and conference hosting with regard to NEPAD and African recovery, but weak on delivery, particularly in its own backyard. In addition, there is, to date, no such thing as a NEPAD project, reflecting limited consensus about what the programme is.

The principal question posed at the start of this paper – whether the conceptualisation of NEPAD is sound, from its philosophical tenets to its organisational structures and relationship with the AU – is thus partly unanswered. This is because there is so much difference between African states, because there is much more clarity required in regard to NEPAD, and because there is still so much to do to change the African developmental condition.

Notes

Acknowledgements

This Adelphi Paper is dedicated
to our teachers, Henry Bienen,
Christopher Clapham and William
Foltz. The concept of this paper
arose from a meeting on
'Governance, Development and the
Logic of African Stability'
organised by the South African
Institute of International Affairs
(SAIIA) in conjunction with the
International Institute for Strategic
Studies (IISS) at Tswalu Lodge in
the Kalahari in 2002. Grateful
appreciation is expressed to
Jennifer and Jonathan Oppenheimer
who sponsored that event.

Introduction

1 See the United Nations
   Development Programme
   (UNDP), Human Development
   Report 2002: Deepening
   Democracy in a Fragmented
   World, (New York: UNDP with
   Oxford University Press, 2002),
   p. 2 and p. 13.
2 For the full text, see www.
   whitehouse.gov/nsc/nss.html
3 For a critique of the Strategy, see

Ivo H. Daalder, James M. Lindsay
and James B. Steinberg, 'Hard
Choices: National Security and
the War on Terrorism', Current
History, vol. 101, no. 659,
December 2002, especially p. 409.
4 See www.state.gov/p/af/rls/fs/
   2001/index.cfm?docid=4004
5 See the United Nations
   Integrated Regional Information
   Network (IRIN), 13 March 2003.
6 *The Economist*, 18 May 2000.

Chapter 1

1 See, in particular, World Bank,
   Can Africa Claim the 21st Century?
   (Washington DC: The World
   Bank, 2000); Shantayanan
   Devarajan, David Dollar and
   Torgny Holmgren, *Aid and Reform
   in Africa: A Report from Ten
   Countries*, (Washington DC: The
   World Bank, 2001); and Nicolas
   van de Walle, *African Economies
   and the Politics of Permanent Crisis,
   1979–1999)*, (Cambridge:
   Cambridge University Press,
   2001).
2 Ibid pp. 7–8.
3 See Carol Lancaster, 'Africa in
   World Affairs', in John W.

Harbeson and Donald Rothchild, *Africa in World Politics: The African State System in Flux*, (Boulder: Westview Press, 2000), p. 212; and Nicolas van de Walle, 'Africa and the World Economy: Continued Marginalisation or Re-engagement?', in Harbeson and Rothchild, *op. cit.*, p. 271.

4   By increasing size, Seychelles, Mayotte, Sao Tomé, Cape Verde, Equatorial Guinea, Comoros, Swaziland, Mauritius, Guinea-Bissau, Gabon, Gambia, Botswana and Namibia.

5   Economic Commission for Africa (ECA), *Transforming African Economies*, (Addis Ababa: ECA, 2001), p. 9.

6   *Ibid.*, p. 12.

7   Human Rights Watch, 'Military Revenge in Benue: A Population Under Attack', April 2002. Available online at www.hrw.org/reports/2002/nigeria/, 31 December 2002.

8   Joshua Forrest, 'State Inversion and Non-State Politics', in Leonardo Villalon and Phillip Huxtable (eds.), *The African State at a Critical Juncture*, (Boulder: Lynne Reinner, 1998), p. 45.

9   Tom Young, 'A Victim of Modernity? Explaining the War in Mozambique', in Paul B. Rich and Richard Stubbs (eds.), *The Counter-Insurgent State: Guerilla Warfare and State Building in the Twentieth Century*, (Basingstoke: Macmillan, 1997), p. 145.

10 See David Keen, 'The Economic Functions of Violence in Civil Wars', *Adelphi Paper* 320, (London: Oxford University Press on behalf of the IISS, 1998).

11 See Rice's testimony to the Hearing on Africa and the War on Global Terrorism before the Subcommittee on Africa of the Committee on International Relations, House of Representatives, 107th Congress, 15 November 2001, Serial No. 107-46. This is available at www.house.gov/international_relations

12 See testimony by Stephen J. Morrison, 'Africa and the War on Global Terrorism', ibid. Morrison contends that: 'Al-Queda cells exist in Cape Town and Durban. Al-Queda has been affiliated with two Cape Town movements, People Against Gangsterism and Drugs (PAGAD) and its associate, Qibla ... The South African government has been too ill-informed, and ill-equipped, to bring effective controls upon radical Islam within its borders'.

13 Rice, Hearing on Africa and the War on Global Terrorism

14 Remarks delivered during the second African Growth and Opportunity Act (AGOA) Economic Forum in Washington DC on 30 October 2002, cited in Ted Range, 'Africa and the War on Terrorism', CRS Report for Congress, (Washington DC: Congressional Research Service, 17 January 2002).

Chapter 2

1   Calculated using the World Bank's World Development Report 1998, (Washington DC: 1998), p. 191.

2   Visit http://web.mit.edu/jeremyp/www/blair.html

3   Susan E. Rice, 'Africa at the Crossroads: The Challenge for the Future', Nairobi, Kenya, 21 November 2000. Available at www.state.gov/www/policy_remarks/2000/001121_rice_kenya.html, 26 December 2002.

4   George W. Bush 'Remarks by the

President on Goree Island.'
Available at www.whitehouse
.gov/news/releases/2003/07/
20030708-1.html

5 Colin L. Powell, 'Remarks at
African Growth and Opportunity
Act Business Roundtable'.
Available online at: www.state.
gov/secretary/rm/2002/
14980.htm, 26 December 2002.

6 See/www.whitehouse.gov/nsc/
nssall.html

7 Available at www.fco.gov.uk, 27
December 2002.

8 Susan E. Rice, 'The Democratic
Republic of the Congo in Crisis',
statement before the
Subcommittee on Africa of the
Committee on International
Relations, House of
Representatives, Washington DC,
15 September 1998. Available
online at www.state.gov/www/
regions/africa/rice_980915.html

9 Colin Powell, 'Remarks at the
University of Witwatersrand', 25
May 2001. Available online at
www.state.gov/secretary/rm/
2001/3090.htm, 31 December 2002.

Chapter 3

1 The authors acknowledge the
assistance of Tim Hughes,
SAIIA's Parliamentary Research
Fellow, in writing this section.

2 Comprising Angola, Botswana,
Democratic Republic of the
Congo, Lesotho, Malawi,
Mauritius, Mozambique,
Namibia, Seychelles, South
Africa, Swaziland, Tanzania,
Zambia and Zimbabwe.

3 Concerns about the pace of
economic delivery are
compounded by the role and the
accessibility of the presidency, a
body that has increased in size
from 27 officials to 330 under
Mbeki. Its budget has risen by

21.6% per annum since 1999,
doubling from R78.7m to R151m
in 2003. It remains not only the
highest decision-making entity,
but increasingly the source of
policy, particularly in the realm
of foreign affairs.

4 For an overview of the South
African economy, see An
Economic Profile of South Africa,
2001, (Johannesburg: Standard
Bank, 2001). For the latest figures,
see The Standard Bank Quarterly
Report at http://196.8.88.70/
research/REV02Q4.PDF

5 See Ernst van Feventer, 'Notes on
the 2000 and 2001 tariff
schedule', available at
www.tips.org.za

6 Foreign direct investment (FDI)
in South Africa from 1994 to 2002
totalled around $22bn, on
average, $2.4bn a year.
BusinessMap cited at 'S. Africa
FDI up in 2002, obstacles remain-
report', www.alertnet.org/
thenews/newsdesk/L1310160

7 See www.whitehouse.gov/nsc/
nssall.html

8 'Mandela criticises the US for its
arrogant approach to Iraq'.
Business Day, 18 December 2002.

9 'Mandela accuses Bush of
seeking global "holocaust"',
Business Day, 31 January 2003.

10 'SA takes a tough stance on Iraq
war', *Saturday Star,* 25 January
2003.

11 'Top ANC man warns US may
target SA next', *Business Day,* 20
February 2003.

12 'ANC dismisses Powell's proof as
"fabrication"', *Business Day,* 6
February 2003.

13 These comments were later
withdrawn. See http://
iafrica.com/news/sa/
196598.htm

14 *Business Day,* 6 November 2002.

15 Speech to the National Council of

Provinces, as reported in 'No dire consequences over Iraq', *Business Day*, 13 November 2002.

16 Nelson Mandela, 'South Africa's Future Foreign Policy', *Foreign Affairs*, vol. 72, no. 5, November–December 1993, p. 88.

17 Finance Minister Trevor Manuel has said with regard to Zimbabwe: 'They say quiet diplomacy has failed. Should we act like Ariel Sharon? Should we? Should we just go in there; kick butt; blow them up; drive over their cars; should we send in our tanks? If there are alternative solutions, let's hear what they are'. Cited in *The Mail and Guardian*, 26 May 2002.

18 'Dlamini-Zuma softens SA stance on Iraq', *Business Day*, 4 March 2003.

19 For details on the conference and its proceedings, visit www.anc.org.za

20 John Battersby, 'A better world is what drives Mbeki's initiatives', *Sunday Independent*, 23 February 2003.

21 *ANC Today*, vol. 3, no. 8, 28 February–6 March 2003.

22 *Sunday Times*, 29 December 2002.

Chapter 4

1 For details see www.nepad.org

2 Jonathan Katzenellenbogen, 'SA's task is to see NEPAD is not an anticlimax', *Business Day*, 15 July 2002.

3 See Jakkie Cilliers, *The NEPAD African Peer Review Mechanism: Prospects and Challenges*, (Pretoria: Institute for Security Studies, 5 November 2002).

4 In terms of the proposals, the APRM is a voluntary process by which member states are subjected to a number of mandatory reviews on political and governance standards. The APRM Secretariat is located within (but in terms of management, operations and funding possibly separate from) the AU Commission and is led by a five to seven member panel of eminent persons. It will apparently involve a number of peer-review teams, comprising elements from, inter alia, the UN's Economic Commission for Africa (UNECA) and the African Development Bank (ADB), the African Parliament, the African Commission on Human and People's Rights and the Economic, Cultural and Social Council (ECOSOC). A two-track approach is increasingly likely, with the UNECA and the ADB focusing on economic and corporate governance reviews, while political governance will be the responsibility of an eminent persons' group, which will appoint specialist institutions/ individuals. See *ibid*.

5 See, Freedom House, 'Freedom in the World 2001–2', available at www.freedomhouse.org/ research/index.htm, and the Heritage Foundation, Index of Economic Freedom 2003, available at www.heritage.org/ research/features/index/

6 Presentation at the South African Institute of International Affairs, 17 September 2002.

7 'Critics ill-informed about NEPAD peer review', *ANC Today*, vol. 2, no. 45, 8–14 November 2002.

8 As of February 2003, these states are Algeria, Angola, Cameroon, Egypt, Ethiopia, Gabon, Ghana, Kenya, Lesotho, Mauritius, Nigeria and Senegal.

9 As noted above, the members of the NEPAD Steering Committee

are: Algeria, Egypt, Nigeria, Senegal and South Africa. These five countries, plus Botswana, Cameroon, Ethiopia, Gabon, Mali, Mauritius, Mozambique, Rwanda, Sao Tomé and Principe and Tunisia formed the original implementation committee. Following a decision taken at the AU summit in Durban, membership of the implementation committee will be increased to 20, with one additional state from each region – thus including Kenya and Libya, given the absence of other regional candidates. Angola has been appointed as the member for SADC, and Ghana as the member for West Africa.

[10] See the G8 Action Plan at www.g8.gc.ca/summitafrica-e.asp

[11] Benin, Burkina Faso, Cape Verde, Côte d'Ivoire, Ghana, Gambia, Guinea, Guinea–Bissau, Liberia, Mali, Niger, Nigeria, Sierra Leone, Senegal and Togo.

[12] Angola, Burundi, Comoros, the DRC, Djibouti, Egypt, Eritrea, Ethiopia, Kenya, Madagascar, Malawi, Mauritius, Namibia, Rwanda, Seychelles, Sudan, Swaziland, Uganda, Zambia and Zimbabwe.

[13] See, for example, Andrew Hill and Peter Speigel, 'Feeling the Heat', *Financial Times*, 8 March 2002 on the implications of the Enron collapse. Such measures are encapsulated within the King Report on Corporate Governance in South Africa. See Deloitte and Touche, *Commentary on the Draft King Report on Corporate Governance in South Africa, 2001*, (Johannesburg: Deloitte and Touche/Institute of Directors, 2001).

Chapter 5

[1] See www.whitehouse.gov/infocus/developingnations/

[2] On the approach and experience of PRSPs, see www.worldbank.org/poverty/strategies/review/

[3] 'The New Partnership for Africa's Development: Origins, Challenges and the Road Ahead', unpublished research paper for the Canadian International Development Agency, 2002.

[4] 'Audit the World Bank', *Financial Times*, 6 March 2002.

[5] See 'Rattling Europe's skeletons', *The Economist*, 16 March 2002.

[6] Available at www.worldbank.org/research/aid/africa/release/aid.htm

[7] Policy was seen in terms of a range of areas: macroeconomic policies (including fiscal, monetary and exchange-rate policies); structural policy (such as tax and trade); public-sector management (including the rule of law, judiciary and social services); and social inclusion/participation.

[8] *New Straits Times*, 27 September 2001.

[9] 'WTO Boss Urges End to Subsidies', *The Nation* (Nairobi), 8 February 2002.

[10] See Bush's statement to the UN Financing for Development Conference, held in Monterrey, Mexico, on 22 March 2002.

[11] Mike Moore interviewed on BBC television, 21 March 2002.

[12] This point was made by Dr Frances Perkins, Executive Director of the Economic Analytical Unit in the Australian Department of Foreign Affairs and Trade (DFAT), at a seminar at the SAIIA on 'Advancing African Agriculture: African-Cairns

Group Partnership',
Johannesburg, 18 March 2003.

[13] Cited in Jakkie Cilliers and
Kathryn Sturman, 'The Right
Intervention: Enforcement
Challenges for the African
Union', *African Security Review*,
vol. 11, no. 3, 2002, p. 29.

[14] 'Africa could redraw map –
Mbeki', *The Citizen*, p. 107, 30
May 2002.

[15] The question is the focus of a
series of conferences organised
by the SAIIA in conjunction with
the Stiftung Wissenschaft und
Politik and Princeton University
in 2002 and 2003.

[16] Charles Tilly, 'Reflections on the
History of European State
Making', in Charles Tilly (ed.),
*The Formation of National States in
Western Europe*, (Princeton:
Princeton University Press, 1975),
p. 38.